CHARACTERS

A one-year exploration of the Bible
through the lives of its people.

VOLUME SEVEN

The Early Church Leaders

LifeWay Press® • Nashville, Tennessee

EDITORIAL TEAM

Brandon Hiltibidal
Director, Discipleship and Groups Ministry

Brian Daniel
Manager, Short-Term Discipleship

Joel Polk
Editorial Team Leader

Michael Kelley
Content Developer

David Briscoe
Content Developer

G.B. Howell Jr.
Content Developer

Rob Tims
Content Editor

Laura Magness
Content Editor

Gena Rogers
Production Editor

Darin Clark
Art Director

Denise Wells
Designer

Lauren Rives
Designer

From the creators of *Explore the Bible*, *Explore the Bible: Characters* is a seven-volume resource that examines the lives of biblical characters within the historical, cultural, and biblical context of Scripture. Each six-session volume includes videos to help your group understand the way each character fits into the storyline of the Bible.

ISBN 978-1-4300-7041-2 • Item 005823509
Dewey decimal classification: 220.92
Subject headings: BIBLE. N.T.--BIOGRAPHY / CHRISTIAN SAINTS

We believe that the Bible has God for its author; salvation for its end; and truth, without any mixture of error, for its matter and that all Scripture is totally true and trustworthy. To review LifeWay's doctrinal guideline, please visit lifeway.com/doctrinalguideline.

Scripture quotations are taken from the Christian Standard Bible®, Copyright © 2017 by Holman Bible Publishers. Used by permission. Christian Standard Bible® and CSB® are federally registered trademarks of Holman Bible Publishers.

To order additional copies of this resource, write to LifeWay Resources Customer Service; One LifeWay Plaza; Nashville, TN 37234; fax 615-251-5933; call toll free 800-458-2772; or order online at LifeWay.com; email orderentry@lifeway.com.

Printed in the United States of America

Groups Ministry Publishing • LifeWay Resources
One LifeWay Plaza • Nashville, TN 37234

CONTENTS

ABOUT EXPLORE THE BIBLE

The Whole Truth, Book by Book

Explore the Bible is an ongoing family of Bible study resources that guides the whole church through the only source of the truth on which we can rely: God's Word. Each session frames Scripture with biblical and historical context vital to understanding its original intent, and unpacks the transforming truth of God's Word in a manner that is practical, age-appropriate, and repeatable over a lifetime.

Find out more at goExploreTheBible.com.

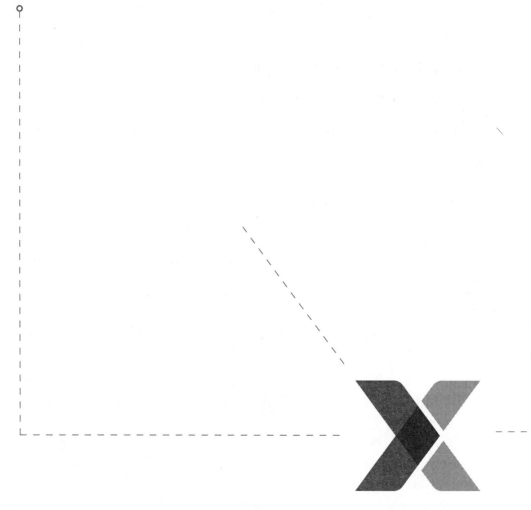

HOW TO USE THIS STUDY

This Bible study includes six sessions of content for group and personal study. Regardless of what day of the week your group meets, each session begins with group study. Each group session utilizes the following elements to facilitate simple yet meaningful interaction among group members and with God's Word.

INTRODUCTION

This page includes introductory content and questions to get the conversation started each time your group meets.

GROUP DISCUSSION

Each session has a corresponding teaching video to introduce the story. These videos have been created specifically to teach the group more about the biblical figure being studied. After watching the video, continue the group discussion by reading the Scripture passages and discussing the questions that follow. Finally, conclude each group session with a time of prayer, reflecting on what you discussed.

BIOGRAPHY AND FURTHER INSIGHT MOMENT

These sections provide more in-depth information regarding the biblical character being spotlighted each session and can be included in the group discussion or personal study times.

PERSONAL STUDY

Three personal studies are provided for each session to take individuals deeper into Scripture and to supplement the content introduced in the group study. With biblical teaching and introspective questions, these sections challenge individuals to grow in their understanding of God's Word and to respond in faith.

LEADER GUIDE

A tear out leader guide for each session is provided on pages 95-106. This section also includes sample answers or discussion prompts to help you jump start or steer the conversation.

The Early Church Leaders

STEPHEN

The Martyred Leader

INTRODUCTION

To believe in Jesus means to stake your life on Him, and the first generation of followers had ample opportunity to test their faith. Stephen was among the first to model a biblical faith in Christ that comes at great cost.

One of the seven men chosen to handle the care ministry to widows, he not only was a compassionate helper, but also a confident witness for Jesus. Stephen spoke the gospel message boldly and persuasively. Some who heard him gave way to an uncontrollable rage, took him outside the city, and stoned him to death, making Stephen the first Christian martyr.

Few, if any, who read this study will be called to die as Christian martyrs like Stephen. Yet his life is an encouragement for all believers to demonstrate courage and confidence when we declare our Christian beliefs and values, even when some risk is involved. The example of Stephen inspires us to exhibit boldness in our own Christian living.

How would those who know you describe your character?

In what ways do you see your character impacting your Christian witness?

Watch the video teaching for Session 1 to discover "The World of Stephen," then continue the group discussion.

GROUP DISCUSSION

FOCUS ATTENTION

Which song title best describes you: "Rock the Boat" or "Peace Like a River"? If you like to keep peace at all costs, what kind of situation would cause you to rock the boat?

EXPLORE THE TEXT

As a group, read Acts 6:8-10.

What uniquely qualified Stephen for his ministry? What do verses 3 and 5 add to your understanding of his qualification? How were those qualities needed for Stephen to do what he did?

As a group, read Acts 6:11-15.

What unfairness did Stephen endure? Once the situation turned hostile, what might Stephen have been tempted to do?

As a group, read Acts 7:51-53.

What accusations did Stephen make against his accusers? Do you think his words were too harsh? Explain.

As a group, read Acts 7:54-60.

Which of these verses elicits strong emotion for you? Why? How is this part of Stephen's story a different kind of boldness than in the previous verses?

APPLY THE TEXT

Through the power and wisdom provided by the Holy Spirit, Stephen didn't back down when opposition arose over his message about Jesus. He continued to do what he had been called to do, even when it meant suffering and death.

Are you willing to ask God to make you bold for the gospel to the point that you will unashamedly share the message of Jesus regardless of the consequences? Why or why not?

What sacrifices is God calling you to make right now for the sake of the gospel?

What does Stephen's martyrdom teach about how God wants us to define success?

Close your group time in prayer, reflecting on what you have discussed.

STEPHEN

KEY VERSES

While they were stoning Stephen, he called out: "Lord Jesus, receive my spirit!" He knelt down and cried out with a loud voice, "Lord, do not hold this sin against them! And after saying this, he died.

— Acts 7:59-60

BASIC FACTS

1. Jewish Christ-follower of Hellenistic (Greek) background; the first Christian martyr.

2. Name *Stephen* is of Greek origin, meaning "crown."

3. Had a reputation of integrity, spiritual maturity, and wisdom.

4. Became an outspoken proponent of the gospel and critic of Jewish legalism.

5. His death precipitated wider persecution of Christians by Saul of Tarsus.

TIMELINE

AD 30–40

- Jesus' ministry, crucifixion, resurrection, ascension 30–33
- Stephen's martyrdom 33
- Birth of the church during Pentecost 33
- Conversion of Saul (Paul) 33

AD 40–50

- Herod Agrippa I rules in Judea 41–44
- Barnabas brings Paul to Antioch 43
- Paul's first missionary journey 47–48
- Jerusalem Council 49
- Claudius expels Jews from Rome 49

KNOWN FOR

1. Stephen was the first among seven well-regarded believers chosen to carry out the early church's widow-care ministry (Acts 6:3-6), a precursor to the church leadership role of deacon.

2. God affirmed Stephen's spiritual power and grace by working miracles through him among the people of Jerusalem (Acts 6:8).

3. Jewish leaders in Jerusalem arrested Stephen, charging him before the Sanhedrin of blasphemy against the temple and the Mosaic law. In his defense, Stephen recounted Israel's long history of rejecting God's chosen deliverers up to and including their recent crucifixion of Jesus Christ (Acts 7:2-53).

4. As the angry mob stoned Stephen to death, this willing martyr prayed for the Lord to forgive his executioners, a group that included a young Pharisee, Saul of Tarsus (Acts 7:58-60).

AD 50-60

- Paul's second missionary journey 50–52
- Paul's third missionary journey 53–57
- Antonius Felix governor of Judea 52–60
- Synoptic Gospels written 55–59
- Paul arrested in Jerusalem; sent to Rome 57–59

AD 60-70

- Paul under house arrest in Rome 61–62
- Apostle James martyred in Jerusalem 62
- Great fire in Rome 64
- Apostle Peter martyred in Rome 66
- Apostle Paul martyred in Rome 67

Stephen: Christian Martyr

By Timothy N. Boyd

The only reliable information concerning Stephen is found in Scripture. Acts 6 portrays him as deeply spiritual. He was one of the seven men the apostles chose to administer the distribution of food to believing Hellenistic widows. Hellenistic Jews were those reared outside Israel in areas dominated by Greek culture. The criteria by which the seven men were chosen also indicates that Stephen was both a highly committed Christian and a recognized leader among the believing Hellenistic Jews. The Book of Acts also indicates that these seven were more than mere administrators; they were heavily involved in spreading the message of Christ.

The events that led to the stoning of Stephen are tied to this Hellenistic background. Stephen had been engaged in debate with members of one of the synagogues that served the Hellenistic Jews (see Acts 6:9-10). He apparently had defeated his opponents in these debates, and they had become jealous and thus plotted against him.

Stephen was charged with blasphemy against the law of Moses, against the temple, and against God (vv. 11-13). These matters were crucial—foundational—to Jewish theology. In his defense, Stephen pointed to many of the ideas that were current among the Hellenistic group in the church. These ideas went beyond the earlier teachings of Peter on the day of Pentecost. Stephen's speech indicates that the coming of the gospel nullified the need for a temple and for the ceremonial law that had built up around the religious activity of the temple. Stephen also recognized that the leadership of Judaism followed historical precedent in opposing the work of Christ.[1]

The biblical text is clear that the ideas Stephen expressed brought on the wrath of the synagogue. The Scriptures do not tell us, however, why Stephen chose to argue boldly his points before the Sanhedrin. It is not likely this early in church history that Stephen was deliberately looking for death as a conscious imitation of Christ. Instead, Stephen was probably following the example laid down earlier by Peter and John. When commanded to stop speaking of Christ, these two apostles replied they had to obey God rather than man and could not stop bearing witness to Christ (see 4:18-20). Thus, Stephen was not seeking death; he was witnessing faithfully to his convictions about

Timothy N. Boyd, "Stephen: Christian Martyr," *Biblical Illustrator*, Summer 1991.

Christ without regard to the consequences. Stephen knew that he had to be faithful in representing Christ to others, even if it meant death. The word *martyr*, in its root meaning, translates as "witness." Stephen was being a faithful witness to Christ. Stephen's death proved to be a forerunner of Christian martyrs through the centuries. The impact of Christian martyrs is not in their deaths—but in their witness.

1. F. F. Bruce, *The Book of Acts* (Grand Rapids: Eerdmans, 1954), 135–36.

The Greek Orthodox Church of St. Stephen dominates the north end of the Kidron Valley at Jerusalem and commemorates the traditional site of the stoning of Stephen, the first Christian martyr.

Illustrator Photo/ Brent Bruce (197/B/0436)

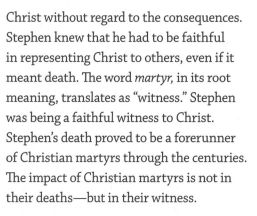

Read Acts 6:1-10.

Starting at Pentecost (Acts 2), the early church experienced explosive growth. But that growth didn't come without challenges; authorities had already arrested church leaders Peter and John (Acts 4), but the growth continued. Now, in Acts 6, the church was presented with a different kind of challenge.

Two cultural groups existed within the church in Jerusalem. The Hellenistic (Greek-speaking) Jews had lived in the Greek-speaking world and culture and migrated back to Jerusalem. The Hebraic Jews resided in Palestine, probably speaking both Aramaic and Greek. The difference between these two groups was more than language; they had different cultures and customs.

A complaint arose among the Hellenistic Jews. They felt that their widows were being overlooked in the daily distribution of food, an organized relief system. Widows with no immediate family to support and care for their daily needs were, in that culture without today's social services, totally dependent on others for survival. Was this discrimination the result of prejudice or resentment? Probably not. In all likelihood, the issue was only an oversight in administration of the system.

A solution was needed. The twelve apostles summoned all the church members to solve the problem. The proposal was to select seven men to serve the needs of the widows. As a result, the apostles were freed to preach the gospel and the church grew (v. 7). Stephen, whose name means "crown," is listed first among these seven. Because his name is Greek, he probably was a Hellenistic Jew who then became a Christian.

We know, however, that Stephen did much more than wait tables. He met the qualifications of being "of good reputation, full of the Spirit and wisdom" (v. 3). Verse 5 reveals he also was "full of faith." Verse 8 adds that he was "full of grace and power." Wisdom, faith, grace, power, and the Spirit's presence marked Stephen as a Christian who was well-equipped for his role.

What adjectives best describe your spiritual life?

Stephen quickly moved beyond waiting tables to giving a powerful witness to the gospel among the Jews. The authenticity of Stephen's ministry was distinguished by "great wonders and signs" (v. 8). The term "wonders" refers to miracles that drew observers' awe and amazement. "Signs" were miracles that gave evidence of God's presence and activity and conveyed spiritual truths. God was working through Stephen in unusual and powerful ways. To this point, only the apostles had performed such deeds.

Synagogues had arisen during the Babylonian exile as centers of worship and education and particularly were devoted to reading and expounding on the law. The Freedman's Synagogue was made up of Cyrenians and Alexandrians as well as some from Cilicia and Asia—one synagogue with four groups. The term "Freedman's Synagogue" indicates these Jews were liberated slaves or descendants of Jewish slaves taken to Rome earlier. As Stephen boldly preached about Jesus, they interrupted him, seeking to refute what he said. They were, however, unable to refute Stephen's message. Through wisdom and the power of the Holy Spirit, Stephen argued effectively against his opponents.

What do you consider the decisive factor in Stephen's ability to best his opponents in this discussion/debate? What implication does this have for you?

We know from chapter 7 that Stephen was wise in the Scripture. We are also told that his opponents couldn't withstand the Spirit by whom he spoke (see 6:10). In the Book of Acts, the Holy Spirit empowered believers for bold witness (Acts 1:8; 2:4; 4:8,31). Later, the apostle Paul told the Corinthians that his preaching was "not with persuasive words of wisdom but with a demonstration of the Spirit's power," so that their faith wouldn't be based on the wisdom of man but on the power of God (1 Cor. 2:4-5). The Holy Spirit still empowers believers today to be bold witnesses of Christ.

How has the Holy Spirit provided you with power to take a stand for Christ?

Read Acts 6:11-15.

Stephen's boldness in standing by his Christian convictions aroused intense hostility. When members of the Freedman's Synagogue were unable to best him in debate (Acts 6:9-10), they brought forward false witnesses against Stephen. The synagogue members either paid these false witnesses or persuaded them, telling them what to say. They contrived a frame-up.

These accusers claimed they heard Stephen speaking blasphemy against Moses and God (v. 11). It's noteworthy that they named Moses before God, almost putting him on a par with God. The phrase "blasphemous words" refers to speech showing disrespect for God and for that which is sacred. To accuse Stephen of disrespecting either the great lawgiver Moses or God Himself was a surefire way to get him into trouble. The penalty for blaspheming God was death by stoning (see Lev. 24:14-16). In our times—when "tolerance" for all speech, respectful or not, is expected and when casual use of God's name in profanity is rampant—it may be hard to imagine someone getting upset because of blasphemous words.

Stephen's accusers stirred up three groups: the people in general; the elders, who were respected leaders and represented the Sadducees; and the scribes, most of whom were Pharisees (v. 12). Elders and scribes made up part of the Sanhedrin, the Jews' high court. They came on Stephen suddenly, seized him forcefully, and took him to the Sanhedrin. This occasion was the third time the Sanhedrin faced followers of Jesus: (1) Peter and John in Acts 4:5-7; (2) the apostles in 5:27-29; (3) Stephen in 6:11-12. The first such trial had ended in a warning (4:21); the second with a flogging (5:40); and the third would end with Stephen's death (7:59-60).

Apparently, the accusers pointed to Stephen's words about the law and the temple (6:13). Stephen likely realized what the sacrificial death of Jesus implied concerning animal sacrifices at the temple in Jerusalem. They are no longer necessary and are obsolete, as the writer of Hebrews later explored in great detail (see Heb. 9–10). Whether Stephen proclaimed this opinion publicly is unknown. We do know he stated publicly that the true worship of God could not be limited to the temple (Acts 7:48-49).

Stephen preached so clearly about Jesus, that the case against him was tied directly to Jesus' teachings (v. 14). Jesus once spoke words that led some people to suppose

He planned to destroy the temple. Early in His ministry, Jesus had stated: "Destroy this temple, and I will raise it up in three days" (John 2:19). But these words were no statement of a plan to attack the temple; rather He spoke about His body. Jesus also had strongly asserted He didn't come "to abolish but to fulfill" the law (Matt. 5:17), although He often interpreted the Scriptures differently than the Jewish teachers did. Jesus did, however, challenge the validity of the oral traditions that had been added to the law. The religious leaders considered these interpretations of the law as sacred as the law itself. Any presumed or real attack on what the Jews regarded as the law would rile them. Thus, the charges that Stephen had spoken against the law were serious.

In a society increasingly hostile to Christian beliefs and values, people may accuse us falsely as believers. We exhibit boldness when we offer Christian beliefs and values as a defense.

What's the difference between Christians offering a defense and being put on the defensive?

Stephen had the full attention of the Sanhedrin. God gave his face a supernatural shining appearance that drew his audience to look intently at him. The Holy Spirit filled Stephen with power for fearless testimony, and the glow of heaven itself was revealed through him. The speech that follows in Acts 7 gives evidence of Stephen's continued boldness. As believers, we are called to exhibit boldness in standing up for Christian beliefs and values even when others are hostile toward our claims.

What pressures do you face to deny or hide the Christian faith?
How does Stephen inspire you to resist those pressures?

Read Acts 7:51-60.

In response to the charges made against him, Stephen gave a lengthy and strong defense of the gospel (Acts 7:2-50). He reviewed Old Testament history, stressing that God could not be confined to one area (the promised land) or to one particular place (the temple). Abraham, Joseph, and Moses experienced God's call and power outside Canaan. With Moses as leader, God delivered the Israelites from Egypt, yet the people rebelled against God, worshiped an idol, and longed to return to Egypt. Through Moses, God had the Israelites build a portable tabernacle to symbolize His presence with them. Only later did Solomon build the temple in Jerusalem. Stephen implied the tabernacle was a more appropriate symbol of God's presence because it wasn't stationary (v. 48). He quoted Isaiah 66:1-2 to emphasize God does not dwell in buildings (vv. 49-50).

What role did Stephen's knowledge of Scripture play in his debate with the Jews? How might a greater familiarity with Scripture help you encounter people who question Christianity? How could you increase your biblical knowledge and awareness?

A strong offense is always a good defense. Stephen described the Sanhedrin members as "stiff-necked" and as having "uncircumcised hearts and ears" (v. 51). The term "stiff-necked" means "stubborn." The Sanhedrin members were proud of their physical circumcision that marked them as members of God's covenant people, but they had failed to take God's revelation of Himself to heart; they had failed to obey Him. As their ancestors had done, the religious leaders persisted in resisting the Holy Spirit.

In what ways could the charges Stephen made against the Sanhedrin be made against you?

In their long history, the Israelites had rejected and killed the prophets—God's spokesmen—who had foretold the coming of Christ (v. 52). When Jesus came as God's promised Messiah, the religious leaders betrayed and murdered Him, thus behaving like their ancestors. Lastly, Stephen referred to the Jewish tradition that God gave the law to Moses through angels (v. 53). Having received the law in the most impressive way possible, the religious leaders had failed to keep it. They broke the law they accused Stephen of speaking against.

The Sanhedrin members couldn't refute Stephen's logical, biblical, and Spirit-empowered words. But they didn't repent and accept the truth Stephen presented. Instead, they gnashed their teeth as an expression of their rage (v. 54).

By the Spirit's inspiration, Stephen received a vision of God's heavenly throne room (vv. 55-56). He saw God's shining brilliance and Jesus standing at the right hand of God—the position of honor, majesty, and authority.

What do you think was the purpose of Stephen's vision of Jesus standing at the right hand of God? How does his vision encourage you?

PAUL

The Missionary Leader

INTRODUCTION

Mention the "Damascus road," and most people familiar with the Bible know you are speaking of the conversion of Saul of Tarsus. Not every conversion is accompanied by flashing lights and a voice from heaven. Several conversion accounts in Acts are without flash or fanfare. For example, the Philippian jailer asked before his conversion, "What must I do to be saved?" (Acts 16:30). The response required only an answer, which was sufficient for him and his household to come to faith.

Why are some conversions more dramatic than others? Although we don't fully know the answer, the context does seem to impact the way God brings a sinner to salvation. Paul, who was known as Saul at the time of his conversion, was "still breathing threats and murder against the disciples of the Lord" (9:1) after the death of Stephen. God used the sights and sounds of the Damascus road to not only get Paul's attention, but to validate His work in Paul among his companions.

Paul's conversion on the Damascus road shouldn't be understood as normative, but as a divine act of God used to prevent many Christians from arrest and martyrdom, and bring Paul to a point of repentance and conversion.

At the end of the day, what is important is not how God speaks, but that you attend to what He says.

In your opinion, which of our five senses would be the worst to lose? Why?

How did the Lord first get your attention? Was it with or without flash and fanfare?

Watch the video teaching for Session 2 to discover "The World of Paul,"
then continue the group discussion.

GROUP DISCUSSION

Focus Attention

Share about a life-changing experience. Describe your life before and after the life change.

Explore The Text

As a group, read Acts 9:1-9.

Take a look at the way Jesus interacted with Saul (Paul) in this passage. Beyond the blinding light, how did He get Saul's attention?

How was Saul (Paul) immediately changed by his encounter with Jesus? How do you think his companions might have responded to the change?

As a group, read Acts 9:10-19a.

The Lord called Saul His "chosen instrument" (v. 15). What does it mean to be chosen by God?

What significant things happened in Paul's life after Ananias prayed for him?

As a group, read Acts 9:19b-21.

In what ways did Paul demonstrate his new commitment to Jesus?

What would people have expected Paul to say when he came to the synagogue? What was the reaction of the people who heard Paul proclaiming the name of Jesus?

APPLY THE TEXT

Saul, while on his way to Damascus to arrest believers, met Jesus and was forever changed. His dramatic conversion story involves a blinding light from heaven, the voice of Jesus, and the restoration of his sight through the ministry of Ananias. However, the transformation of Saul the persecutor to Paul the proclaimer of Christ was the greater miracle. Jesus is still in the business of changing lives.

Do you assume some people are beyond God's reach? How does the account of Saul's conversion challenge those assumptions?

Recall a time when God got your attention. What were the circumstances?

Who is someone in your life, like Ananias, who has helped you on your spiritual journey?

Close your group time in prayer, reflecting on what you have discussed.

PAUL

KEY VERSES

But the Lord said to him, "Go, for this man is my chosen instrument to take my name to Gentiles, kings, and Israelites. I will show him how much he must suffer for my name."

— Acts 9:15-16

BASIC FACTS

1. Prominent young Pharisee who became a believer in Christ and went on to become the early church's leading gospel proponent, theologian, church planter, and writer of Scripture.

2. Name *Paul* is of Greek origin, meaning "small" or "humble"; Hebrew name, *Saul,* means "asked for."

3. Born in Tarsus, capital of Roman province of Cilicia; thus held Roman citizenship along with Jewish heritage (tribe of Benjamin).

4. Had occupational skills as a tentmaker.

5. Received rabbinic training in Jerusalem under Gamaliel, a prominent rabbi.

6. Died a martyr in Rome, probably at the decree of Emperor Nero.

TIMELINE

AD 30–40	AD 40–50
Jesus' ministry, crucifixion, resurrection, ascension 30–33	Herod Agrippa I rules in Judea 41–44
Birth of the church during Pentecost 33	Barnabas brings Paul to Antioch 43
Stephen's martyrdom 33	Paul's first missionary journey 47–48
Conversion of Saul (Paul) 33	Jerusalem Council 49
	Claudius expels Jews from Rome 49

KNOWN FOR

1. Before his own conversion, Paul was an ultra-zealous Pharisee who believed God wanted him to persecute Jews who had become Christians (Acts 9:1-2; 22:3-4; 26:9-11).

2. Paul was converted to faith in Jesus Christ after a dramatic encounter with the risen Lord on the road to Damascus (Acts 9:3-19).

3. More than any other Christian leader of his day, Paul developed church planting and strengthening as a model for gospel expansion and fulfilling the Great Commission. Further, God inspired Paul to write much of the New Testament including letters to several churches and to several coworkers.

4. Paul endured numerous instances of suffering for the gospel, including floggings, beatings, imprisonments, stonings, and personal hardships (2 Cor. 11:24-27).

5. God appointed Paul to be an apostle (Rom. 1:1; Gal. 1:1); he came to be known as "the apostle to the Gentiles" because of his focus on preaching the gospel of salvation by grace through faith to both Jews and Gentiles on his missionary journeys.

6. Paul was one of the primary participants and spokesmen at the first church council (Acts 15:12).

AD 50–60	AD 60–70
Paul's second missionary journey 50–52	Paul under house arrest in Rome 61–62
Paul's third missionary journey 53–57	Apostle James martyred in Jerusalem 62
Antonius Felix governor of Judea 52–60	Great fire in Rome 64
Synoptic Gospels written 55–59	Apostle Peter martyred in Rome 66
Paul arrested in Jerusalem; sent to Rome 57–59	Apostle Paul martyred in Rome 67

From Persecutor to Persecuted

By Cecil Ray Taylor

Repeatedly in his letters, Paul confessed his earlier persecution of Christians (see Gal. 1:13,23; 1 Cor. 15:9; Phil. 3:6). Under his Jewish name, Saul, Paul guarded the garments of Stephen's accusers as they threw the first stones to kill him (see Acts 7:58). Enthusiastically, he joined an organized attack against Christians at Jerusalem (8:3). With authority from the high priest, he arrested and imprisoned followers of Jesus and brought them before synagogue courts where he "tried to make them blaspheme" (26:11), that is, to deny Jesus, and punish them if they refused.

Once he became a Christian, however, Paul found the persecution he used to inflict on Christians was now aimed at him! A selective list of his "sufferings" is in 2 Corinthians 11:23-28. Among other things, the apostle claimed he was in "many more imprisonments" than the false apostles who were his target (2 Cor. 11:23). The Acts record shows Paul was incarcerated four times: Philippi (16:23), Jerusalem (22:23–23:32), Caesarea (23:33–26:32), and Rome (28:16-31). Probably he was released from his Roman imprisonment and had a later period of ministry. Later he was re-arrested (2 Tim. 1:8), although no one knows why or when, and held in Rome, likely until Nero had him beheaded.

Also Paul wrote he was beaten "many times near death" (2 Cor. 11:23). Five times from Jewish authorities he received thirty-nine lashes, as prescribed in the Mishnah (*Makkoth* 3:10). Three times Roman authorities beat the apostle with rods (11:25). Once, at Lystra, people stoned the apostle and left him for dead (Acts 14:19).

The Lord said His disciples would be banned from the synagogues (John 16:2a). The Gospels confirm that early Christians were, in fact, excluded for confessing Jesus of Nazareth as God's Messiah (John 9:22; 12:42; 16:2). The Jewish community also had milder forms of exclusion. Just one person could punish others for religious or moral offenses by simply refusing to talk to them for a month. A more severe punishment took away all religious privileges for an indefinite period. Most severe was complete and final expulsion of the victim from the entire Jewish community. The Scriptures do not indicate whether Paul imposed such exclusionary acts or experienced them himself.

The hill in the center is the site of ancient Lystra, which has never been excavated. After healing a man who had been crippled, the crowds at Lystra tried to worship Paul and Barnabas. The two protested and directed the praise to God. Incensed at the crowd's reaction, Jews from Iconium and Antioch came to Lystra and persuaded the citizens to stone Paul, drag him out of town, and leave him for dead.

Illustrator Photo/ Bob Schatz (12/10/4)

Jesus promised that believers would be blessed "when they insult you and persecute you and falsely say every kind of evil against you because of me" (Matt. 5:11). "Persecute" hints at physical attack; "insult" and "falsely say all kinds of evil" describe verbal assaults. The Master said: " 'A servant is not greater than his master.' If they persecuted me, they will also persecute you" (John 15:20). Such a warning reminds us that we should not be surprised if, within our lifetimes, we who are Christians in America pay for our faith by experiencing physical persecution. If that happens, we can be reassured, knowing we will be entering more fully into "the fellowship of [Christ's] sufferings" (Phil. 3:10).

Cecil Ray Taylor, "Saul the Persecutor, Paul the Persecuted," *Biblical Illustrator,* Winter 2009-10.

Read Acts 9:1-22.

No individual's transformation by the gospel recorded in the Book of Acts is more dramatic than that of Saul of Tarsus, also known as Paul. He went from being a merciless persecutor of Christians to arguably the church's most passionate and effective missionary, theologian, and writer of Scripture.

Acts 9 picks up the thread of a story introduced in 8:1-3. After briefly spotlighting Philip's ministry, Luke resumed the account of the persecution Saul led against Christians. Saul intended to imprison the messengers of Jesus and thereby silence their message about Jesus. He secured documents of authority from the high priest in Jerusalem so that he could arrest believers living in Damascus and extradite them to Jerusalem (9:1-2).

At this point in the story, we know how misguided Saul was. He was sincere, but he was sincerely wrong. He needed the new life found only in Jesus Christ. The beginning of Saul's transformation from persecutor to apostle began with Christ's appearance to him on the road as he neared Damascus.

A blinding light from heaven and the voice of Jesus interrupted Saul's journey to Damascus. Jesus asked Saul why he was persecuting Him, and told him to get up and go into Damascus where he would receive further instructions (9:3-9). Saul thought he was going to Damascus to give orders; instead he would arrive in the city to receive orders that changed him forever.

At the same time, God commanded a believer named Ananias, who lived in Damascus, to go to the house where Saul was staying and pray for him. There are many Christians who quietly serve the Lord behind the scenes. Their names seldom appear in the news or in history books, but their obedience to God often shapes the future in remarkable ways. Such a believer was Ananias, whom the Lord sent to instruct and baptize Saul.

Ananias had heard about Saul's hostile activities against believers in Jerusalem and knew that Saul had come to Damascus with the same intent. He was hesitant to go and find Saul (9:13-14). The Lord explained that Saul was His chosen instrument to carry His message to Gentiles, kings, and the Israelites. Ananias obeyed the Lord. He found Saul and prayed for him. Saul immediately regained his sight and was baptized.

Who in your life, like Ananias, has helped you on your spiritual journey?

Bible students sometimes debate the precise time that Saul was saved. Some hold that it happened on the Damascus road. Others suggest it occurred during the three-day period in Damascus (9:11). Still others propose that Saul's conversion happened during Ananias's visit. What we can know with absolute certainty is that Jesus saved and changed Saul, forgiving him of his sin. The Holy Spirit filled Saul and began to prepare him for the great work of taking the gospel to the ends of the earth.

Saul's baptism in verse 18 was an act of obedience and his public profession of being a follower of Jesus Christ. His baptism signaled the end of his fasting. Not only was Paul's eyesight restored, but he also regained his strength. Equally important, he gained spiritual strength by meeting for several days with the disciples in Damascus (v. 19). Soon after, Saul began testifying about Jesus in the synagogues and proclaiming Jesus as the Son of God and the Messiah (9:20-22). No doubt many of the Jews who heard Saul proclaim Jesus wondered how a fervent-hearted Pharisee could change so radically in his message.

Why was it significant that Saul immediately began to proclaim Jesus?
Why do new believers often display passion for telling others about Jesus?

In what ways does your life reflect your relationship with Christ?

Read Acts 14:1-23.

God revealed His purpose for Paul to Ananias first: "This man is my chosen instrument to take my name to Gentiles" (Acts 9:15). Several years had passed when the Holy Spirit directed the church at Antioch to set apart Barnabas and Saul for missionary work among the Gentiles (13:1-3). The first of three missionary journeys of Paul is recorded in Acts 13:4–14:28.

After traveling through Cyprus and Antioch of Pisidia, Paul and Barnabas made their way to Iconium (14:1). Again, they entered the Jewish synagogue (see also 13:14). As in Antioch of Pisidia, the proclamation of the gospel created division among the people (14:2; see also 13:48-50). The gospel has a way of dividing people based on their acceptance or rejection of the message. When it was discovered that those opposing Paul and Barnabas were planning to harm them, they fled to Lystra, sharing the gospel along the way (14:3-7).

In Lystra, God used Paul to heal a crippled man (vv. 8-10), just as He had used Peter to bring about the healing of a man sitting by the temple gate called Beautiful in Jerusalem (Acts 3:2-8).

How does God use people today to accomplish His work? How does that compare to how He used Paul in this passage?

When the crowd saw what Paul had done, they didn't pat him on the back and say, "Praise God." Instead, because their city was full of statues to the Greek gods, they thought he and Barnabas were Hermes and Zeus. A popular story in Roman folklore told of Jupiter and his son Mercury disguising themselves and walking through this region. The story tells of them seeking shelter, only to be rejected until a poor elderly couple took them in. It concluded with the couple being rewarded and those who rejected them being punished. The people of Lystra understood the coming of Paul and Barnabas to be a visit from their mythical gods.

How would this experience have been a test of what truly motivated Paul and Barnabas? What attitudes did Paul and Barnabas display in pointing the people to Jesus?

Barnabas and Paul were grief stricken when they saw the misguided response from the crowd. Refusing to be the focus of the people's worship, they instead tried to point the crowd to the one true God who alone is worthy of worship and praise.

Just when it seemed that the situation had calmed down, Jews came from other cities, determined to stop Paul at all costs. These visitors convinced the people of Lystra to join them in the mob action of stoning Paul. Rocks hit Paul with enough force that he fell to the ground as if dead. The groups assumed they had killed him and drug his body outside the city (v. 19).

Instead of immediately leaving the area, Paul went back into the city. The next day he and Barnabas left for Derbe. The stoning didn't discourage them from completing their mission. After evangelizing and making many disciples in Derbe, Paul and Barnabas began their return to Antioch, their home base. Along the way, they stopped in several towns they had previously visited—Lystra, Iconium, and Antioch of Pisidia—to encourage disciples in their faith and warn them of troubles to come (v. 22).

Paul and Barnabas weren't the only Christians to have troubles because of their faith. Historians tell us that most of the apostles were killed because of their stand for Christ. God's Word doesn't say that we might have persecution. It says that we will. It is imperative for us, as believers, to be ready for it.

What can we learn from Paul's response to his opponents that might help us deal with efforts to discredit or quiet the gospel message today?

Read Acts 28:16-31.

In the second half of Acts (chs. 13–28), Paul made three missionary journeys, explained his conversion on multiple occasions, was imprisoned, hailed as a god, stoned, left for dead, and faced trumped-up charges and threats on his life. The Book of Acts ends with Paul in custody in Rome and awaiting trial before Caesar. The thread that connects all these events is that Paul saw every circumstance as an opportunity to share the gospel.

Paul's normal pattern was to begin work in a new city by visiting the Jewish synagogue. Since he was under house arrest in Rome, he invited the local Jewish leaders to come to him (28:17). Paul's imprisonment began with Jews in Jerusalem charging him with teaching against the Jewish law and the temple (21:28). So Paul began his address to the Jews in Rome by stating that he had done nothing that could be understood as being against the law or against his own people. He explained that his innocence was affirmed by the Roman leaders, but the objections of Jews present at his hearing caused him to appeal to Caesar (25:9-11). The Roman authorities in Judea had no choice but to send Paul to Caesar (26:30-32). As a Roman citizen, he had the right to have his case heard by Caesar.

The reason Paul wanted to visit with the Roman Jewish leaders was to tell them about the hope he had found in Christ (28:20). The hope of Israel centered on the fulfillment of the Old Testament promises, and Paul firmly believed that Jesus was the promised Messiah.

God uses a variety of means to bring believers in contact with others who need to know the gospel. We should be looking to share the gospel with all people, especially those who are seeking to know more. Ask God to help you be more attentive to opportunities to share the gospel this week.

Though they didn't know Paul's specific case, the Jewish leaders in Rome had heard about Christianity. Emperor Claudius had expelled Jews from Rome in AD 49 on the charge they were creating disturbances because of Christ (see Acts 18:2). After Claudius's death in AD 54, Jews began to return to Rome, including those who had become Christians. The Jewish leaders Paul addressed appear to have kept their distance from those who had become Christians, but they were curious and open to hearing him teach and arranged a second meeting with him.

What makes the gospel message so intriguing and interesting? How does that intrigue open the door to share the gospel with others?

The second meeting between Paul and the Roman Jewish leaders lasted a full day (28:23). Because they were Jewish, Paul focused attention on how Jesus fulfilled the Old Testament. He explained the Old Testament—the Law of Moses and the Prophets—through the lens of Jesus' life, death, and resurrection (v. 23). Some were convinced by what Paul said, but others refused to believe (v. 24). Most of the Jewish community in Rome continued to oppose Christianity.

How does the gospel divide and unite at the same time? Why does the gospel have this kind of effect on people?

Paul still had a desire to see his own people come to faith in Christ (Rom. 9:1-3). But he also realized there were Gentiles who were waiting and willing to respond to the gospel (Acts 28:28). It was to these Gentiles that Paul had been sent in the first place.

The Book of Acts ends by stating that Paul remained in Rome two more years under house arrest, preaching and teaching about the gospel with boldness and without hindrance. Paul was fulfilling God's purpose for his life—he was taking the gospel to the Gentiles.

How does verse 31 set the stage for how your life could become a continuation of the Book of Acts?

BARNABAS

The Encouraging Leader

INTRODUCTION

It is a great honor to be assigned the role of "minister of encouragement" for other believers. The early church Christian who set the standard for all Christian encouragers was Barnabas. Barnabas's given name was Joseph. The apostles in Jerusalem recognized his encouraging nature and nicknamed him Barnabas, which means "Son of Encouragement" (Acts 4:36).

Barnabas consistently displayed the quality of encouragement. He facilitated Paul's acceptance by Jerusalem believers (9:26-28). He affirmed and encouraged the new believers in Antioch, and he mentored Saul by enlisting him to help in the ministry there (11:22-26). He later stood up for John Mark when Paul refused to allow Mark to accompany them on the second missionary journey (15:36-41).

The recurring picture of Barnabas in the New Testament is of one who went out of his way to encourage others. This pattern of encouragement serves today as a model for believers to follow.

Did you have a nickname as a child? If so, what was it and why was it given to you?

Who would you say has been the greatest encourager in your life? In what way?

Watch the video teaching for Session 3 to discover "The World of Barnabas," then continue the group discussion.

GROUP DISCUSSION

FOCUS ATTENTION

Do you look at the glass as half-empty or half-full? Why? Who is the most positive person you know? What does he or she do to make you think that?

EXPLORE THE TEXT

As a group, read Acts 11:19-22.

Why might the church in Jerusalem have sent Barnabas to Antioch?

As a group, read Acts 11:23-24.

Other than the fact that he had the reputation of being an encourager, what about Barnabas led the church at Jerusalem to select him to report to them?

As a group, read Acts 11:25-26.

Knowing Barnabas's character, why do you think he recruited Paul's help? What work was there for Barnabas and Paul to do in Antioch?

As a group, read Acts 11:27-30.

What fears could have gripped the church on hearing the news from Agabus? What happened instead?

Does it seem strange to you that a young church would send aid to one that is already established? Explain. What does this fact tell you about the Christians in Antioch?

APPLY THE TEXT

Barnabas played a key role at a critical crossroads in the growth and expansion of the New Testament church. People like Barnabas are always needed by the church. They seek no glory for themselves but only seek to bring out the best in others.

In the early stages of your relationship with Christ, who encouraged you to persevere? How did he or she do that?

In what way(s) can you encourage a new believer or new church member this week?

In what way(s) can you follow the example of verses 27-30 this week and help a fellow believer who is in a difficult situation?

Close your group time in prayer, reflecting on what you have discussed.

BARNABAS

KEY VERSE

When he arrived and saw the grace of God, he was glad and encouraged all of them to remain true to the Lord with devoted hearts.

— Acts 11:23

BASIC FACTS

1. Jewish Christian leader in the early church who befriended new believer Saul (Paul) and later accompanied him on his first missionary journey.

2. Given name was *Joseph* (Acts 4:36); name *Barnabas*—likely a nickname—of Aramaic origin, meaning "Son of Encouragement."

3. Born into a Levite family, thus received training in Scripture as a child.

4. Became a follower of Christ soon after the resurrection and ascension, if not before.

5. Age and circumstances of his death unknown; named as author/hero of several apocryphal works from later centuries.

TIMELINE

AD 30–40

- Jesus' ministry, crucifixion, resurrection, ascension 30–33
- Birth of the church during Pentecost 33
- Stephen's martyrdom 33
- Conversion of Saul (Paul) 33

AD 40–50

- Herod Agrippa I rules in Judea 41–44
- Barnabas brings Paul to Antioch 43
- Paul's first missionary journey 47–48
- Jerusalem Council 49
- Claudius expels Jews from Rome 49

KNOWN FOR

1. Barnabas was known for generous character. He sold a plot of his land to help provide for needy Christians in the early church (Acts 4:36-37).

2. He championed Paul's salvation experience by accompanying and introducing Paul to the apostles in Jerusalem as a changed man (Acts 9:27).

3. Church leaders in Jerusalem sent Barnabas to Antioch to confirm great evangelistic results there. Barnabas then recruited Paul to join him in the gospel work at Antioch (Acts 11:20-26).

4. Barnabas and Paul were set apart by the Antioch church to take the gospel message to Cyprus and the central Anatolian regions of Pamphylia and Pisidia, the first missionary journey (Acts 13–14). John Mark accompanied the team as far as Perga, but then returned to Jerusalem.

5. Barnabas accompanied Paul to the first church council in Jerusalem, confirming the many conversions of Gentiles to the faith (Acts 15:12).

6. At the start of the second missionary journey, Barnabas had a falling out with Paul over whether to allow John Mark to come with them. The two Christian leaders decided to part ways and form two teams. Barnabas and John Mark traveled back to Cyprus (Acts 15:36-39).

AD 50–60

- Paul's second missionary journey 50–52
- Paul's third missionary journey 53–57
- Antonius Felix governor of Judea 52–60
- Synoptic Gospels written 55–59
- Paul arrested in Jerusalem; sent to Rome 57–59

AD 60–70

- Paul under house arrest in Rome 61–62
- Apostle James martyred in Jerusalem 62
- Great fire in Rome 64
- Apostle Peter martyred in Rome 66
- Apostle Paul martyred in Rome 67

Barnabas: All We Know

By Roy E. Lucas, Jr.

Barnabas was born into a Levitical family from Cyprus. Originally named Joseph, the apostles in Jerusalem nicknamed him "Barnabas" ("Son of Encouragement," Acts 4:36). The early church saw in Barnabas "a good man, full of the Holy Spirit and of faith" (11:24). Several actions gave evidence of those traits. Barnabas sold a field and gave the profit to the church (4:36-37). He bore the title "apostle" (14:14). He intervened for Paul when the Jerusalem disciples and apostles expressed concern about the former persecutor (9:26-27). Barnabas embraced John Mark when Paul rejected him as a partner for mission work (15:36-41). He supported Paul against some Judeans who wanted to force circumcision on the Gentile believers as part of salvation (Acts 15; Gal. 2:1-10). No other man in the New Testament demonstrated such consistent encouragement to his associates.

Barnabas's Personality

Barnabas frequently worked with apostles and evangelists. He ministered with Paul about two years (Acts 11:25-26; chs. 13–15). Their names are linked over twenty times in the New Testament. Barnabas also spoke and acted on behalf of others. He intervened on Paul's behalf when the apostle needed an introduction to the leadership in Jerusalem. When facing the Jerusalem Council concerning the issue of Gentiles coming to faith in Christ, Barnabas supported Paul by contending that God saved Gentiles without them having to undergo circumcision (see ch. 15). Later, preparing for the second missionary journey, when Paul adamantly refused to take John Mark, Barnabas so cared for John Mark that he split with Paul and took John Mark with him to Cyprus (vv. 36-39).

Barnabas's Gifts

Barnabas was a gifted preacher and teacher. The church in Antioch of Syria recognized his gifts as he ministered there over a year, and then as they commissioned him by the guidance of the Holy Spirit to take the gospel to other people (11:26; 13:1-4).

Barnabas equipped the saints for the work of the ministry. He found Paul, who was in Tarsus, and brought him to Antioch to help teach (11:25-26). He teamed with Paul on the first missionary journey and sailed to his homeland of Cyprus. Perhaps prior to

Roy E. Lucas, Jr., "Barnabas: All We Know," *Biblical Illustrator*, Fall 2012.

their leaving, he had worked with Paul in developing the strategy of launching their work from the local synagogues (13:4-5). He re-engaged John Mark in the work after his initial failure (15:36-39).

Barnabas's Strengths

Barnabas exemplified what it meant to prefer other believers above himself (see Phil. 2:3). He willingly shared leadership with Paul. He humbled himself by working to support himself (see 1 Cor. 9:6). He yielded the content of his preaching to the Jerusalem church elders so they could examine it.

The Jerusalem church recognized Barnabas's trustworthy character as being strong enough to represent them to the church of Antioch. The Antiochian believers expressed confidence in Barnabas by sending their love offering to the Jerusalem church by him. Additionally, this church commissioned Barnabas and Paul to carry the gospel into Asia Minor. Barnabas's encouraging model for a Christ-centered life serves as a pattern for today's believers to follow.

The south Hellenistic city gate at ancient Perga in Asia Minor (modern Turkey). It is flanked by two large defense towers. Perga was the major city of the ancient region of Pamphilia in Asia Minor. Paul and Barnabas passed through this city (Acts 13:13-14; 14:24-25). Young John Mark returned from this ancient port to Jerusalem.

Illustrator Photo/ David Rogers (5/11/9)

43

Read Acts 4:32-37.

The opening verses of Acts 4 relate the story of Peter and John's arrest. Annoyed by the apostles' preaching about Jesus, the Sadducees took Peter and John into custody and brought them before the Sanhedrin, who ordered them to stop preaching about Jesus (vv. 1-18). Peter countered that the disciples would obey God, not man (vv. 19-20). After threatening the apostles further, the Sanhedrin released them (vv. 21). Peter and John returned to the gathered believers, and the whole assembly prayed for boldness to continue proclaiming the good news of Jesus.

With the Jewish council's intimidating demands, the early believers in Jerusalem might have worried about the financial stability of their families if they faced persecution, arrest, or even death. Yet in the face of opposition and threat, the church continued in unwavering commitment to the mission of God and to one another. The phrase "of one heart and mind" in verse 32 conveys the idea of harmony and oneness of purpose and devotion to Christ.

What does it look like when a church is "of one heart and mind"? What are some examples of this kind of unity in your church?

The fellowship of the early church was marked by an unselfish sharing of material possessions. Believers "held everything in common" (v. 32). Followers of Christ refused to claim their rights of possession and gave liberally of what they had to meet others' needs. The believers viewed themselves as partners in a glorious enterprise and supported one another generously.

Openly defying the Sanhedrin's orders not to preach about Jesus, the disciples continued to proclaim Christ as the living Savior. Their testimony centered on Jesus' death and triumphant resurrection. These were essential elements in the message the early believers proclaimed. That "great grace was on all of them" (v. 33) implies the people's favorable response to the apostles' witness concerning Jesus.

Verse 34 continues the account of the Jerusalem believers' solidarity by reporting there was not a needy person among them. The reason was that from time to time property owners sold their holdings and brought the proceeds to the apostles (v. 35). The express purpose of sharing material goods was to meet people's needs, and genuine needs actually were met. Out of a deep sense of unity came generous sharing to help others.

Sharing financial resources is a way to meet others' physical needs, but it also expresses Christian love and promotes unity in the church. Sharing our financial resources with others gives evidence of the Holy Spirit's work in our lives. Giving money, however, does not preclude personal involvement.

At this point in the story, Luke gave a specific example of one believer's generous sharing (vv. 36-37). Joseph (also called Barnabas) sold some land and gave the money to the apostles to be used for needy believers. Barnabas became a prominent leader in the early Christian church with his name appearing twenty three times in Acts and five times in Paul's letters.

Why do you think Luke included in this account the actions of Barnabas? How could Barnabas's gift have been an encouragement to others?

Barnabas's gift served as a practical example and encouragement for other early believers. Those who had needs were encouraged by knowing he really cared about them. Those who had resources were encouraged to follow his example and give of their resources to meet others' needs. We also can be inspired and motivated by Barnabas's example as we understand that one way we can encourage others is to be generous to support the Lord's work of meeting people's needs with our finances.

How would your life be different if you were as generous as Barnabas?

Read Acts 9:26-27; 15:36-41.

If there was a person the early believers had a right to be wary of, it was Saul of Tarsus. When an angry mob stoned their friend Stephen to death, Saul had given his approval (see Acts 8:1). In the intense persecution that followed Stephen's death, Saul was at the forefront, determined to snuff out Christianity by any means necessary (see 8:3; 9:1-2). He was a real threat to anyone who trusted in Jesus.

But then something happened. On Saul's way to arrest Christians, he met Jesus. Blinded for days, Saul regained his sight when a believer named Ananias came to disciple and baptize Saul. He then began to preach what He previously fought against (9:20). Saul naturally wanted to get to know other disciples and learn from them. They naturally were not so eager. The disciples had legitimate reasons for distrusting Saul. Enter Barnabas. Barnabas recognized God's working in Saul's life, befriended him, and vouched for him as he brought him into the group. New Christians need people to recognize real change and come alongside them. You might be just the one God is calling to welcome a new believer into the church family.

What risk did Barnabas take by vouching for Saul? What do you suppose he saw in Saul?

Eventually, Saul and Barnabas became a great ministry team; they began to travel from town to town sharing the gospel and building up the church (13:1-3). But they didn't always agree. As the two prepared for their second missionary journey, Barnabas wanted to bring along John Mark (15:36-37).

John Mark was Barnabas's cousin (see Col. 4:10). He was also the son of Mary, in whose house the church was meeting when Peter was miraculously freed from prison (see Acts 12:12). John Mark had been a companion of Barnabas and Saul, now Paul, on their first missionary journey. But Mark didn't complete the journey; he instead had returned to Jerusalem (13:13). Because of this, Paul didn't think it was a good idea to take John Mark on their second journey (15:38).

Because of their disagreement over John Mark, Paul and Barnabas parted ways. Barnabas took John Mark with him and sailed to Cyprus, while Paul chose Silas and went another direction (15:39-41). After Paul and Barnabas parted company, Barnabas never reappears in the Book of Acts. The reason for this must be related to Luke's purpose in writing the book. He was writing to explain to Theophilus how the gospel spread across the Roman Empire, eventually coming to Rome (Acts 1:1). Therefore, Luke's focus was naturally on the apostle Paul.

The ongoing impact of Barnabas, however, can be measured in part by the useful role John Mark would play in God's mission following this incident in Acts 15. John Mark is believed to be the writer of the Gospel of Mark. Paul also later recognized and valued John Mark's usefulness (see Col. 4:10; 2 Tim. 4:11; Philem. 23-24). John Mark was one of Paul's fellow workers who sent greetings when Paul wrote the Book of Philemon (Philem. 24). Paul also wrote to the Colossians to receive Mark if he came to them (Col. 4:10), and when Paul wrote his final letter to Timothy, he asked Timothy to bring Mark with him because Paul considered Mark a useful helper (2 Tim. 4:11).

Barnabas played a key role in helping John Mark fulfill God's plan for his life. Barnabas vouched for Paul when no one else trusted him. Barnabas was equally passionate about mentoring John Mark when others had no confidence in him.

Based on these passages, how would you describe Barnabas's contributions to the work of the early church?

What are you doing that reflects your God-given purpose?

Read Acts 11:19-30.

Once again, we see Barnabas doing Barnabas-like things. Recall that the name Barnabas was a nickname meaning "Son of Encouragement" (Acts 4:36). We have seen examples of why Joseph earned this name: the generous sharing of his resources (4:37); vouching for Saul the former persecutor (9:26-27), and embracing and mentoring John Mark (15:37-41).

The events in Acts 11:19-20 are significant in Luke's story of the expansion of the gospel—both geographically and culturally. Stephen's murder led to the scattering of Christians. Those who were scattered initially preached the gospel only to Jews (v. 19). We know that by this time some non-Jews had heard and accepted the gospel—the Ethiopian official (8:26-40) and Cornelius the Roman centurion (ch. 10), for example. The Ethiopian and the centurion, however, were God-fearing Gentiles—meaning they already had embraced the Jewish religion.

In Antioch, a new thing was happening. Jewish believers began evangelizing Greeks who apparently had no connection to Judaism. When they heard the good news of Jesus, a large number of these Greeks believed (11:21). News of this successful evangelization reached Jerusalem, and Barnabas was sent to Antioch (v. 22).

Given what you already know about Barnabas, why do you think he was sent to Antioch?

Barnabas rejoiced when he saw all that was happening, and he encouraged the new Christians to stay true to the Lord (v. 23). Barnabas's encouraging the Antioch church had decisive significance for the development of the early church. In the next verse, Luke added a note about the character of Barnabas: "He was a good man, full of the Holy Spirit and of faith" (v. 24).

Not only did Barnabas encourage and teach the new believers, many more people came to Christ after Barnabas arrived (v. 24b). Barnabas understood a key principle—wise leaders know when they need help from others. He knew he couldn't effectively disciple this many new believers by himself. He left Antioch briefly to find Saul and enlist him to join him in ministry. Previously Saul needed Barnabas (Acts 9:26-28); now Barnabas needed Saul. Saul was still a fairly young Christian at this point; his days as the great Christian role model, Paul, were in the future.

How was Barnabas an encouragement to Saul (Paul) by asking him to accompany him to Antioch to help teach the people?

Luke repeated the words "large numbers" in verses 24 and 26 as he told how Barnabas made a deliberate effort to mature the church. First, large numbers were evangelized. Then large numbers of new believers were taught the faith over the course of a year.

"The disciples were first called Christians at Antioch" (v. 26). "Christian" may have been used as a term of ridicule. However, Luke's noting that believers were called Christians in Antioch indicates that the evangelizing and teaching of the new believers made a strong impact on the city in a short time and that others recognized the Christ-centered nature of the believing community.

During the time Barnabas and Saul ministered in Antioch, some traveling preachers arrived from Jerusalem. One was a prophet named Agabus, to whom the Spirit revealed that a great famine would spread throughout the whole Roman world (11:28). In light of this predicted hardship, the new believers in Antioch determined to send relief to the Christians living in Judea. By means of Barnabas and Saul, the Antioch believers sent their gifts to the Jerusalem church (vv. 29-30).

Barnabas had a reputation of putting action with his faith. Previously, he encouraged needy Jerusalem believers by selling his property and donating funds (4:36-37). Consistent with his character, he now demonstrated concern for the Jerusalem believers by leading others to join him in helping and encouraging them.

JAMES

The Unifying Leader

INTRODUCTION

Most have a love-hate relationship with rules. No one ever gets old enough or powerful enough to be exempt from rules. Rules can make us feel secure; they give us a level of comfort. But rules can easily become the main thing—the object of our focus.

As Christians, we must keep our focus on the main purpose we have—telling others about Jesus. If we aren't careful, our attention can be turned inward to ourselves or to our fellow church members. If that happens, we can quickly allow our focus to drift toward rule-keeping. After all, keeping rules is like having a scorecard. We have something against which we can measure our "performance" or compare ourselves to others. Before we realize it, the attention is on us, and not on the main purpose we have in this life—to know Christ and make Him known. This was a problem that the first-century church faced, too.

James, as the leader of the Jerusalem church, was instrumental in keeping the church focused on the main thing.

How do you feel about rules?

When have rules caused you to lose sight of what's really important?

Watch the video teaching for Session 4 to discover "The World of James," then continue the group discussion.

FOCUS ATTENTION

What are some of the rules you're expected to follow in your daily routine? What are some of the "extra-biblical" rules we place on new believers?

EXPLORE THE TEXT

As a group, read Acts 15:1-5.

Who came to Antioch from Jerusalem, and what were they teaching? How did Paul and Barnabas respond, and what did the church propose?

As a group, read Acts 15:6-11.

What significance did the gospel being inclusive of different people groups have for the Jews? the Gentiles?

As a group, read Acts 15:19-23.

What was James's recommendation? How did his judgment satisfy both parties?

What is the significance of the four actions prohibited?

As a group, read Acts 15:30-31.

The messengers arrived in Antioch and read the letter, reporting the council's decision. How might the letter (recorded in vv. 23-29) have been encouraging to Gentile believers (v. 31)?

APPLY THE TEXT

James's knowledge of Scripture (vv. 13-18), sensitivity to the Holy Spirit (v. 28), and leadership role in the church made him the right person to lead the church to confront this challenge that could have derailed it's faithfulness to the gospel message and obedience to the Great Commission.

Are there any signs that your church or Bible study group has turned its focus inward, instead of focusing on people who are far from God? What are those signs?

How might you or your church unintentionally make it harder for a believer who has just turned to Christ?

What lessons can you learn from James about dealing with distractions that take the church's focus off the main thing—the gospel?

Close your group time in prayer, reflecting on what you have discussed.

JAMES

KEY VERSE

Therefore, in my judgment, we should not cause difficulties for those among the Gentiles who turn to God.

— Acts 15:19

BASIC FACTS

1. Half-brother of Jesus who became leader of the church in Jerusalem after Simon Peter.

2. Name *James* is Greek form of Hebrew name *Jacob*, meaning "supplanter" or "trickster."

3. Oldest of four biological sons (and at least two sisters) born to Joseph and Mary after Jesus' miraculous birth while Mary was a virgin (Matt. 13:55-56).

4. Became known as "James the Just" for his consistently fair and righteous character.

5. Led the Jerusalem church until his martyrdom around AD 66 (according to later church tradition).

TIMELINE

AD 30–40

- Jesus' ministry, crucifixion, resurrection, ascension 30–33
- Birth of the church during Pentecost 33
- Stephen's martyrdom 33
- Conversion of Saul (Paul) 33

AD 40–50

- Herod Agrippa I rules in Judea 41–44
- Barnabas brings Paul to Antioch 43
- Paul's first missionary journey 47–48
- James presides at Jerusalem Council 49
- Claudius expels Jews from Rome 49

KNOWN FOR

1. James and his siblings were skeptical of Jesus' messianic identity and mission until after the crucifixion (Mark 3:21; John 7:2-5).

2. Paul stated that one of Jesus' resurrection appearances was to James (1 Cor. 15:7). Paul specifically sought out the acceptance and counsel of Peter and James following his conversion (Gal. 1:18-19).

3. As the leader of the Jerusalem church, James presided over the first church council, expressed his judgment that Gentiles were not to be hindered from the gospel, and participated in drafting a written statement to this effect to be sent to the church in Antioch (Acts 15:13-29).

4. James met with Paul in Jerusalem after the third missionary journey in an unsuccessful effort to help Paul mollify his Jewish detractors in the city and avoid arrest (Acts 21:17-25).

5. James is most likely the writer of the New Testament epistle of that name (Jas. 1:1).

AD 50–60

- Paul's second missionary journey 50–52
- Paul's third missionary journey 53–57
- Antonius Felix governor of Judea 52–60
- Synoptic Gospels written 55–59
- Paul arrested in Jerusalem; sent to Rome 57–59

AD 60–70

- Paul under house arrest in Rome 61–62
- Great fire in Rome 64
- Death of James, Jesus' half-brother 66
- Apostle Peter martyred in Rome 66
- Apostle Paul martyred in Rome 67

James: All We Know

By Robert E. Jones

James grew up in Nazareth and later lived in Capernaum. Until shortly after Jesus' resurrection, James, along with his siblings, was an unbeliever. James's conversion to belief in Jesus as the promised Messiah took place after experiencing the Lord's personal appearance to him after His resurrection (1 Cor. 15:7). This post-resurrection appearance then placed James among the earliest witnesses to Jesus' resurrection.

James stands tall as a person of influence in the New Testament church. Our first encounter with him in the Book of Acts finds James and his brothers as part of the group awaiting the Holy Spirit's coming at Pentecost (Acts 1:14). The picture we find here describes a spirit of oneness among Mary and her sons as they joined those gathered for prayer.

Four subsequent events paint a clear picture of James's influence in the early church. First, by around AD 44, and during the time of Peter's imprisonment and deliverance (12:6-19), James had evidently become head of the Jerusalem church. After Peter's miraculous release from prison, he instructed those who had been praying for him to make a report of "these things to James and the brothers" (v. 17). This statement implies James had become a recognized authority in the Jerusalem church.

Second, in Galatians 1:18-20 Paul stated that three years after his conversion, he went to Jerusalem to see Peter (Acts 9:26-30). During that visit Paul indicated he saw none of the other apostles except James. Once again James is singled out—evidently he was a leader among the apostles.

Third, during the Acts 15 conference (15:6-29) James took a mediating role between Paul and the Judaizers. At James's initiative the council drafted a letter to the Gentile believers placing minimal requirements on them. By siding with Paul in the controversy, James exerted influence upon the council that effectively defeated the Judaizers.

Finally, when Paul returned to Jerusalem at the conclusion of his third missionary journey (Acts 21:17-25), he met with "James, and all the elders" (v. 18), who rejoiced after hearing of Paul's work among the Gentiles (v. 20). Because of a common view among the Jews that Paul was a law-breaker (v. 21), James and the elders suggested

Robert E. Jones, "James: All We Know," *Biblical Illustrator*, Fall 2018.

that Paul should demonstrate his attention to ritual matters. He could do so by paying for the sacrifices of four men who had completed their Nazirite vows. James brought up the idea, not because he thought Paul was a law-breaker, but because others who were zealous for the law believed it. We can conclude from this event that James possessed a zeal for the law and a consideration for not offending the many thousands of believing Jews (v. 20).

In his epistle, James defends works as an essential means for demonstrating genuine faith. Indeed, he had lived that life of works. A concluding summary statement of James's prominence in the New Testament church is in Galatians 2:9, where Paul listed James first among Cephas and John as "pillars" of the church.

Overview of modern Nazareth; the large structure in the center with the conical roof is the Church of the Ascension, which, according to tradition, marks the spot where the angel appeared to Mary. Nazareth was the hometown of Mary and Joseph and thus the place where James would have grown up.

Illustrator Photo/ Brent Bruce (60/9794)

Read Galatians 2:6-10.

Three people in the New Testament bear the name James. First, there is James the apostle, the brother of John and son of Zebedee. Second, James the son of Alphaeus was one of Jesus' twelve apostles. He is also known as James the younger. The third James, the one most likely referred to in Galatians as "the Lord's brother" (Gal. 1:19), is listed among the brothers of Jesus in Mark 6:3.

James wasn't a follower of Jesus during His earthly life. With the exception of His mother, apparently none of Jesus' earthly relatives accepted His claim to be the Messiah prior to the resurrection. Paul records that Jesus made a special post-resurrection appearance to James, and he is listed among the witnesses to the resurrection in 1 Corinthians 15:7.

James became a member of the church at Jerusalem and among the 120 who witnessed the outpouring of the Holy Spirit on the day of Pentecost (see Acts 1:14; 2:1). He quickly rose to a position of leadership within the Jerusalem church and is one of the most important characters in the history of the early church. In Paul's Letter to the Galatians, he indicated that James, along with Cephas (Peter), and John, was one of the "pillars" of the church (Gal. 2:9) and was among those who were "recognized as important" (v. 6).

After the apostle Paul founded churches in the Galatian region, some men had come preaching circumcision and obedience to the ceremonial law as necessary for salvation. Paul wrote Galatians to emphasize faith in Christ alone as necessary for salvation.

The main topic addressed in Galatians is the same as what was debated at the Jerusalem Council in Acts 15—that circumcision or other religious works were not necessary for salvation. Paul accused the Galatians of deserting the gospel of salvation by grace through faith in Christ and turning to a works-oriented salvation (see Gal. 1:6). The Galatians weren't saying Jesus was unnecessary, but they were implying He wasn't enough. They claimed that faith in Christ had to be accompanied by certain Jewish rituals.

In Galatians 2:1-10, Paul wrote that he and Barnabas went to Jerusalem to explain how the Lord was saving Gentiles without requiring circumcision (2:3). In verse 9, he mentioned the three key leaders who confirmed his call to go to the Gentiles: James,

Peter, and John. These spiritual pillars in the church had the responsibility to serve Christ by leading the church to remain loyal to the saving mission of God.

James, Peter, and John extended to Paul the "right hand of fellowship" (v. 9), a common sign of acceptance and agreement. They agreed that Paul should continue preaching the gospel to the Gentiles, just as they would continue their work among the Jews.

Whose work was more important, Paul's ministry to the Gentiles or the work of James, Peter, and John among the Jews? Explain.

In God's eyes, there is no difference between Jews and Gentiles. He intends the good news about Jesus to be shared with all people. Some people groups, however, will not hear the gospel unless Christians follow God's call to leave their comfort zones and cross geographical, cultural, and other barriers to proclaim the gospel.

Where is God calling you to step into His mission of making the gospel known to all people? How are you being faithful to what God is calling you to?

The only request James, Peter, and John made of Paul was that he remember the poor, which Paul had made every effort to do (v. 10). Caring for the poor was an important priority in the early church, and it was important to James. James warned the church to stop dishonoring the poor by treating others better than them (Jas. 2:1-6). Real faith causes us to be involved, not indifferent.

Read Acts 15:1-29.

After their first missionary journey, Paul and Barnabas remained in Antioch. During their stay, some men traveled from Judea to Antioch and began to teach that Gentiles must be circumcised to be saved (v. 1). Paul and Barnabas contested the Judaizers' teaching that circumcision was necessary for salvation—that Gentiles had to be a part of Israel, the covenant community, to become Christians. Paul and Barnabas rejected the Judaizers' claim in a heated, face-to-face confrontation. Then, possibly in a called meeting, the church at Antioch formally designated Paul and Barnabas and some others as representatives to go up to the apostles and elders in Jerusalem to settle this matter.

The apostles and elders of the Jerusalem church gathered to consider the problem (v. 4). The issue under consideration was whether Gentiles had to be circumcised and keep the law of Moses in order to be saved. Peter spoke first, affirming that Gentiles are saved in the same way Jews are saved—by grace through faith in Jesus (vv. 6-11). When Peter went to Cornelius's house (ch. 10), God provided the Gentiles an opportunity to receive the gospel. After Peter, Barnabas and Paul spoke, describing all the signs and wonders God had done through them among the Gentiles (v. 12).

Because James presided over the meeting, he spoke last (v. 13), calling for the assembly's attention. Doubtless all ears were attuned to him because of his position as leader of the Jerusalem church. His task was to sum up the discussion.

Why is it important in any controversy to look to the Scriptures for guidance?

James quoted from the prophets Amos and Isaiah to support his case. Amos 9:11-12 foretold Israel's restoration "so the rest of humanity may seek the Lord—even all the Gentiles who are called by my name" (Acts 15:17). James also quoted Isaiah 45:21 to stress that long ago God had announced His intention to offer Gentiles His grace. Scripture, of course, is our supreme source of wisdom when we face conflict.

What role should Scripture play in resolving a conflict within a church or between two believers?

James announced his opinion, perhaps as a formal motion: Gentiles would not have to become Jewish converts to become Christians (v. 19). Then he suggested a letter be sent to Gentile churches instructing believers to keep four ritual requirements in deference to Jewish Christians. By being sensitive to the beliefs and practices of Jews, Gentile Christians might reach them (vv. 20-21).

The Jerusalem church's leaders and the whole church agreed with James's opinion (likely by vote), and they took steps to implement it (v. 22). They wrote a letter and selected men from the church to travel to Antioch with Paul and Barnabas (vv. 23-29). These men could interpret and explain the letter to the Gentile churches.

What kinds of spiritual questions are being asked in the church today? What can you learn from James about the way a church should handle potentially divisive spiritual questions?

When the believers in Antioch read the letter from James and the other leaders, they were glad for its encouraging message. They rejoiced that their salvation in Christ was affirmed. They rejoiced that the gospel they had believed was correct, that salvation is a result of grace alone, not grace plus works. Also, they no doubt were glad they didn't have to begin the process of becoming Jewish proselytes, which all Gentile believers would have been required to do if the Judaizers' position had been affirmed.

Read Acts 21:17-26.

Paul and his party arrived in Jerusalem with a collection from Gentile churches to help needy Jerusalem Christians (Acts 24:17; 1 Cor. 16:1). He hoped these funds would heal the growing breach between Jewish and Gentile believers.

The following day, Paul visited James and the Jerusalem church's elders (v. 18). James was the Jerusalem church's leader. Paul went into detail about his latest missionary endeavors, emphasizing what God had accomplished among the Gentiles through his ministry (v. 19). James and all the elders praised God but quickly moved to a "however." They pointed out how many thousands of Jews had become Christians (v. 20). The church leaders likely were referring to the success in evangelizing Jews in Jerusalem and Judea. Many of the Jewish converts may have been Pharisees, who meticulously kept the law, including the oral tradition surrounding it.

The new Jewish Christians had been told about Paul (v. 21). Probably Jews who had been scattered abroad brought reports concerning Paul to Jerusalem. More than merely informing Jerusalem Jews about Paul, the returnees were highly critical of him. They accused Paul of teaching all the Jews who were among the Gentiles to abandon the law of Moses (v. 21). Furthermore, the accusers said Paul was telling Jews to stop circumcising their sons. He purportedly was advising Jews not to live by their ancient practices. Although the church's leaders didn't give credence to the charges, they felt Paul needed to counter the criticisms.

James suggested some practical steps Paul could take so the non-believing Jews could see that he did still abide by Jewish law, even though he was a believer in Jesus Christ (vv. 23-25). If Paul took these actions based on adherence to Jewish law, such Jews would see that the rumors about him were false.

James and the elders explained to Paul that four men had taken a vow, probably a temporary Nazirite vow (v. 23). The leaders urged Paul to join the four men and to purify himself along with them. A Nazirite vow extended for 30 days. During the 30 days of the vow, the men did not eat meat or drink wine; and they let their hair grow. At the period's completion, they would offer costly sacrifices: a lamb, a ram, a basket of unleavened bread, cakes of fine flour and oil, a meat offering, and a drink offering. Then their heads would be shaved and the hair would be burned as an offering.

How were James's suggestion and Paul's actions expressions of humility and love?

Paul's acts would show his faithfulness to the law. James's plan for Paul may seem complicated to us; but in the first century, those familiar with a Nazirite vow as a part of Jewish law and piety understood James's suggestion perfectly.

How do you decide when you should bend for the sake of others and when you should stand firm for your principles? Where would you draw the line?

Paul's actions didn't compromise his convictions. Rather, his actions acknowledged Jewish believers' right to keep the law. The ceremonial rites had nothing to do with salvation. Paul was acting on the principle that he wrote about in 1 Corinthians 9:20. Furthermore, he wanted to strengthen relationships between Jewish and Gentile believers.

We may face unfair criticism for a variety of reasons, and it may distort what we believe or do. When it happens, we can seek to be wise like James and take positive actions that will help disprove unfair criticism against us while not compromising our convictions.

If you were asked to change your behavior to help win unbelievers or to help disciple new believers, what would you do? What would your choice reveal about you?

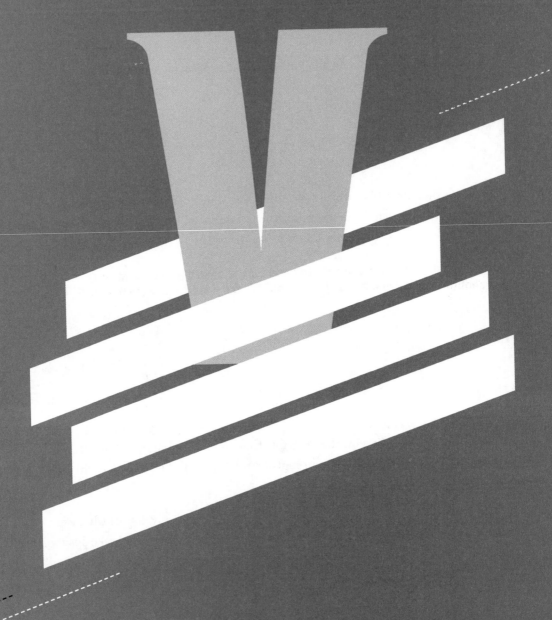

PRISCILLA AND AQUILA

The Servant Leaders

INTRODUCTION

As you look back over the course of your life, you can likely point to specific people who shaped you into the person you are today. Chances are these people of influence were not public figures you watched from afar; but individuals with whom you had a personal connection—people who invested in you.

In the Book of Acts, Priscilla and Aquila stand out as people who used their influence well in this regard. Their platform wasn't a stage, but their home and even their business. They invested in people—like Paul. They employed the apostle in their tentmaking trade and opened their home to him. They even risked their lives for him. They took the eloquent Apollos aside, perhaps into their home, and filled in the gaps in his theological understanding. In Corinth and also in Rome, they invited the church to meet in their home.

The husband and wife team of Priscilla and Aquila were ordinary Christians with whom we can identify and imitate. Within our sphere of influence are people who know Christ but need assistance and encouragement, like Paul. Others are genuine Christians but lack doctrinal clarity on a particular matter, like Apollos. Perhaps we know others who have no understanding of the gospel, or some who have heard the gospel but refuse to believe in Christ.

The story of Priscilla and Aquila shows us how ordinary people can impact lives and have significant influence in the work of Christ and His church.

What ordinary people would you point to today as having significant influence in God's work?

How does your work put you in a place to share Jesus with others and represent Christ?

Watch the video teaching for Session 5 to discover "The World of Priscilla and Aquila," then continue the group discussion.

FOCUS ATTENTION

In what subject would you be a good tutor? In what subject do you feel inadequate? Explain.

EXPLORE THE TEXT

As a group, read Acts 18:24-26.

What words give you clues about Apollos's skills and giftings? What are the different ways believers respond to people who are confident and gifted communicators?

What concern did Priscilla and Aquila have with Apollos and his teaching?

What can we learn from the way Aquila and Priscilla confronted Apollos?

Why is a limited understanding of the gospel and the Christian faith a dangerous proposition?

As a group, read Acts 18:27-28.

How did God use the church in Ephesus to minister to Apollos?

What was the end result of Priscilla and Aquila's actions on behalf of Apollos?

APPLY THE TEXT

This account of Priscilla and Aquila reveals to us a great deal about Christian teaching in the early church. Apollos's previous instruction "in the way of the Lord" reflected the early church practice of teaching new converts basic truths concerning Jesus. The spontaneous instruction of Apollos in the home of Aquila and Priscilla, however, shows that Christian teaching was not restricted to "official" teaching in the church. Aquila and Priscilla—not preachers but tent-makers by trade—contributed to Apollos's spiritual growth and thus to the ongoing mission of the church by their willingness to involve themselves in his life.

If someone came to you with an incomplete understanding of Christianity, would you help him or send him to someone else? Why?

What gifts do you feel you might have that God has given you for Christian service? Where do you sense God has equipped you to serve?

Close your group time in prayer, reflecting on what you have discussed.

PRISCILLA AND AQUILA

KEY VERSE

He began to speak boldly in the synagogue. After Priscilla and Aquila heard him, they took him aside and explained the way of God to him more accurately.

— Acts 18:26

BASIC FACTS

1. Christian couple from Italy who met and evangelized with Paul in Corinth and later in Ephesus.

2. Name *Priscilla* is of Roman origin, meaning "ancient, venerable"; also written as *Prisca* (2 Tim. 4:19).

3. Name *Aquila* also of Roman origin, meaning "eagle."

4. Aquila was born in Pontus, a region of north-central Anatolia along the southern coast of the Black Sea.

5. Tentmakers by trade.

TIMELINE

AD 30–40	AD 40–50
Jesus' ministry, crucifixion, resurrection, ascension 30–33	Herod Agrippa I rules in Judea 41–44
Birth of the church during Pentecost 33	Barnabas brings Paul to Antioch 43
Stephen's martyrdom 33	Paul's first missionary journey 47–48
Conversion of Saul (Paul) 33	Jerusalem Council 49
	Aquila and Priscilla forced to leave Rome 49

KNOWN FOR

1. Aquila and Priscilla likely were Jewish, since they left Rome because of Emperor Claudius's decree in AD 49 that expelled all Jews from the city (Acts 18:2). Whether they became Christians before or after meeting Paul in Corinth is unclear, but they were surely believers by the time they accompanied Paul from Corinth to Ephesus (Acts 18:18-19).

2. While in Ephesus, the couple successfully mentored Apollos, an Alexandrian Jew who fervently taught the truth about Jesus as the Messiah, but did not fully understand some other elements of the gospel (Acts 18:24-26).

3. Aquila and·Priscilla evidently returned to Rome after the death of Claudius and organized a church congregation in their home. Paul greeted them in his Letter to the Romans and acknowledged the couple had risked their lives for him (Rom. 16:3-5).

4. The couple may have relocated again to Ephesus near the end of Paul's life, perhaps to assist Timothy in leading the Ephesian church (2 Tim. 4:19).

AD 50-60

- Aquila and Priscilla join Paul in Corinth 50
- Paul's third missionary journey 53–57
- Antonius Felix governor of Judea 52–60
- Synoptic Gospels written 55–59
- Paul arrested in Jerusalem; sent to Rome 57–59

AD 60-70

- Paul under house arrest in Rome 61–62
- Apostle James martyred in Jerusalem 62
- Great fire in Rome 64
- Apostle Peter martyred in Rome 66
- Apostle Paul martyred in Rome 67

Paul's Means of Support

By Timothy Faber

Sitting in a Roman prison, writing to the Philippians, Paul expressed overwhelming gratitude for the generous gift they had sent for his support (Phil. 4:15-18). The Philippians were showing solidarity and fellowship with Paul through their generous gift. Knowing that they remembered him and cared for him was more valuable to Paul than the gift itself.

From the time he met Christ on the road to Damascus, until his death as a martyr, Paul was supported by his own hands as a tentmaker, by gifts from his church, and probably even through patronage. During Paul's early adult years as a persecutor of Christ-followers, and later during the years between his conversion and Barnabas calling him to Antioch, Paul would have supported himself by making tents. He also returned to this trade several times in his ministry as a follower of Christ and missionary, clearly doing so while in Corinth (Acts 18:3). At Corinth, Paul met Aquila and his wife Priscilla, who were also tentmakers. Paul stayed with them and worked with them for about eighteen months (v. 11). When he left Corinth for Syria, Aquila and Priscilla accompanied him and went as far as Ephesus.

Being imprisoned for long periods of time prevented Paul from plying his trade as a tentmaker and certainly led to his willingness to accept the gift the Philippi church sent. Ultimately, though, Paul's desire in regard to his ministry and his relationship with the churches was that he not be a burden to any of them.

Understanding Paul's first mission partner's background and character may give insight to another source of funding for the apostle's ministry. Soon after Pentecost a man from Cyprus by the name of Joseph sold a tract of land and gave the proceeds to the church. This man was also a great encouragement to the Jerusalem church and earned the nickname Barnabas (see 10:36). Barnabas was later sent to Antioch to investigate the reports of Greeks turning to Christ, and Barnabas was the one who went to Tarsus to enlist Paul's help with the work in Antioch (11:22-24).

When Paul set out on his first missionary journey, Barnabas accompanied him. Barnabas seems to have been more than just a traveling companion to Paul. As they were ministering in Lystra, a lame man was healed when Paul commanded him to

Timothy Faber , "Paul's Means of Support," *Biblical Illustrator*, Winter 2016-17.

stand. That the crowd associated Barnabas with Zeus and Paul with Hermes indicates that at this point people viewed Barnabas as the superior, associating him with the chief pagan god, and Paul, the lesser (Acts 14:11-12). Thus Barnabas being Paul's patron, at least in the beginning of his missionary work, is a strong probability.

Throughout his ministry, Paul did have multiple revenue streams. Nothing indicates, though, that he was ever wealthy. Whether by receiving patronage, working with his own hands in a secular trade, or accepting the occasional gifts of the churches, Paul ensured the gospel was preached freely to those who needed to hear it.

The bema (tribunal) where Paul stood before Gallio in Corinth (Acts 18:12-17). In the background is Acro-Corinth. When Aquila and Priscilla became Christians is unclear, but they may have become Christ followers at Corinth through Paul's gospel message. Like Paul, they too were tentmakers.

Illustrator Photo/ Bob Schatz (11/8/12)

Read Acts 18:1-3.

Chapters 13–21 of Acts describe the apostle Paul's three missionary journeys. Paul and his coworkers took seriously the Great Commission to share the gospel to the ends of the earth, making disciples as they went. Acts 18:1-23 details the conclusion of the second journey, which included: adding Timothy (16:1-3) and probably Luke to the team; an undeserved beating and jail time in Philippi leading to the conversions of a jailer and his family (16:22-34); a riot in the city of Thessalonica after many came to faith in Jesus (17:1-9); and an unusual opportunity in Athens to share the gospel with Greek philosophers at the Areopagus, or Mars Hill (17:16-34). Paul led many people to faith in Christ as he moved from place to place.

Of significance is the fact that Paul didn't work as a lone ranger but formed ministry teams. Among the coworkers with whom Paul formed a deep bond that lasted many years was the husband and wife team of Priscilla and Aquila. Acts 18:1 tells of Paul first meeting this couple when he arrived in Corinth from Athens.

Who are the Christian friends and coworkers with whom you share your life and do ministry? If you don't have any such friends, how can you change that?

Aquila, a Jew, came from Pontus, a province in the northeastern region of Asia Minor along the Black Sea between Bythynia and Armenia. His wife Priscilla (Prisca) was likely a Roman citizen. The couple had traveled from Rome when the Roman emperor Claudius expelled the Jews from Rome in AD 49 because of riots arising in the Jewish community.

We aren't told whether Aquila and Priscilla were Christians before they met Paul. Most likely, they were already believers by the time Paul met them in Corinth. Aquila was a native of Pontus, and citizens of Pontus were in Jerusalem on the day of Pentecost (Acts 23:9). Therefore, we know Christianity spread to Pontus early. It is also possible that Aquila and Priscilla had come to faith in Christ while in Rome. In the event they were not believers before they met Paul, they surely were believers when Paul left Corinth.

Like Paul, Aquila and Priscilla worked as tentmakers. Some have speculated that they owned a tentmaking business, with branches in Rome, Corinth, and Ephesus. Aquila and Priscilla gave Paul a place to live and work in Corinth (18:3).

Paul wrote often about his "secular occupation" and seemed to take a good bit of healthy pride in his self-support (1 Cor. 4:12; 1 Thess. 2:9; 2 Cor. 11:7). Only here, however, does the Bible tell us Paul was a tentmaker, working either in leather or cilicium, cloth woven from goat's hair. Willingness to work to support oneself while proclaiming the gospel was a life principle for Paul. Perhaps this came from his rabbinic days when students were required to adopt a trade so they need not depend upon teaching for a livelihood. Paul's tentmaker job was a means to an end for him to travel and spread the gospel message. During his time in Corinth, Paul shared the gospel in the midst of his day-to-day life and work.

People with similar interests and occupations can cooperate together to forward the progress of the gospel. Do you have friends with whom you share common interests? How can you use those common interests in God's work?

Christians don't have to give up their jobs to be effective in God's service. How could your present job be a vehicle for you to engage in God's kingdom work?

Read Acts 18:24-28.

When Paul left Corinth, Priscilla and Aquila traveled with him to Ephesus (18:18-19). That's where the couple met Apollos, who was sharing the message of Christ in the synagogue. As a visiting Jewish teacher, Apollos would have been invited to speak. As Jewish Christians, Priscilla and Aquila still worshiped in the synagogue.

Apollos was an eloquent speaker and a cultured, learned man. He was well versed in the Old Testament (v. 24) and had been instructed in the way of the Lord (v. 25). Apollos was a native Alexandrian of Egypt, which had a large Jewish population. Jews from Egypt were present at Pentecost, and some who became believers may have taken the gospel back to Alexandria.

What Apollos said in the synagogue was accurate, but it was incomplete because he knew only the baptism of John. John's baptism indicated repentance, symbolized an inner cleansing, and anticipated the Messiah's coming. Christian baptism pictures Jesus' death and resurrection. It symbolizes the believer's dying to sin and being raised to new life. Apollos's lack of understanding likely was an incomplete grasp of Christian baptism.

What questions might people with an incomplete understanding of Christianity ask? What should we do if we can't answer them?

Priscilla and Aquila recognized a deficiency in Apollos's presentation. When Aquila and Priscilla heard Apollos's teaching in the synagogue, they knew immediately that they wanted to have a hand in his spiritual growth. Someone had taught him well the way of the Lord because he already had a good grasp of the Scriptures and the way of the Lord, but he still needed someone to teach him more.

Spiritual growth isn't knowing more about the Bible, it is becoming more like Christ. In what ways do you make an effort to continue to grow spiritually?

The missionary couple took Apollos home with them, and they picked up where his previous teachers had left off in his instruction, so he could become an even stronger believer. Priscilla and Aquila filled in the gaps in Apollos's knowledge of Jesus' life and ministry—and perhaps what had transpired since His resurrection.

This is all we are told about what Priscilla and Aquila did for Apollos, but their investment in his life led Apollos to have a fruitful ministry in Corinth and probably elsewhere. After receiving instruction from Priscilla and Aquila, Apollos crossed over to Achaia, where Corinth was located (v. 27; see also 19:1). He began a productive ministry in Corinth, strengthening the Christians there. His success demonstrated the effectiveness of the extra teaching he had received from Priscilla and Aquila.

Thorough knowledge of the Hebrew Scriptures and skills in interpreting them enabled Apollos to demonstrate Jesus was the Messiah. This was a remarkable incident, and it shows the kind of people Priscilla and Aquila were. What married couple hears a young preacher, notices something lacking in his message, and invites him to their home as an act of Christian hospitality and as a time to teach the preacher? Priscilla and Aquila knew their Bible and the Christian gospel. They were sensitive enough to offer help. And they were hospitable and bold.

Do you know a young Christian with enthusiasm and zeal who needs more training in the basics of Christian faith? How could you help that person?

Read Romans 16:3-5.

In Paul's letter to the Roman Christians, he included the names of believers there to whom he wanted to send his greetings (Rom. 16). Paul named twenty-six people in verses 3-16. Some have argued that Paul couldn't have known so many in a church he had never visited. However, the many who are named here may have been Paul's friends, converts, and coworkers in other places who had moved to Rome. Since he had never been to Rome, he would have been eager to greet the ones he knew.

Why is it important that we have close Christian friends? Why is it important that we have coworkers in ministry? What purpose do these groups serve? What do we miss out on when we try to go it alone?

Priscilla and Aquila were the first to be greeted. Clearly, Priscilla and Aquila's loyalty to Christ had not diminished across time. Years earlier, Paul met them in Corinth, where he stayed and worked with them (Acts 18:2-3). When he set sail for Ephesus, they went with him (18:18-19). They had opened their home to Apollos so they could help him grow in Christ (18:26). Now years later in Rome, where they evidently had moved, they had a church meeting in their home (Rom. 16:5). Wherever they moved, there was a church meeting in their house (Rom. 16:5; 1 Cor. 16:19).

Whether you are married or single, what are some ways your home could be more like the home of Aquila and Priscilla?

The normal first-century pattern was for congregations to meet in private homes for instruction and prayer (see Acts 2:42-47; Col. 4:15). The church consists not of bricks and mortar; it is an assembly of believers in Christ. The growth of the church is not dependent upon buildings erected for the specific purpose of worship.

Verse 4 tells of an event not recorded elsewhere in the Bible. Paul mentioned a time when these two friends had saved his life by risking death themselves. The most likely time this happened was during the riot in Ephesus when Paul had to leave the city (Acts 19:23-41). This may have been in the same crisis Paul described in 1 Corinthians 15:32, recalling that he "fought wild beasts at Ephesus." Whenever it happened, these friends laid their lives on the line to deliver Paul from danger. Paul remembered it and put it into his Letter to the Romans and thus into God's Word. This not only showed them his love and gratitude, but also showed the Roman church his high regard for these two. Jesus said, "No one has greater love than this: to lay down his life for his friends" (John 15:13).

In what areas of life should you be willing to take risks for God, as Priscilla and Aquila did?

Paul paid further tribute to this Christian couple when he wrote the last part of verse 4. He said that not only did he give thanks for them, but also all the churches of the Gentiles were thankful for Priscilla and Aquila. We know of churches in three cities in which this dedicated pair had made a difference for good and God—Corinth, Ephesus, and Rome.

In Paul's final reference to Priscilla and Aquila in 2 Timothy 4:19, they were again in Ephesus. What is noteworthy about Priscilla and Aquila is that wherever they went, they served Christ and His church faithfully. When they moved from one city to another, they carried their faith with them.

Study all the Scripture references to Aquila and Priscilla, and you will notice an interesting detail about them and their marriage. In every reference, they are mentioned together as a couple. Neither Luke nor Paul ever wrote about them separately. The consistency in the way they were identified in the New Testament testifies to the joint commitment to Christ that they shared in ministry. They provide an excellent example of how Christian couples can serve the Lord together to make a huge difference in kingdom work.

TIMOTHY

The Young Leader

INTRODUCTION

If you had to turn over your business or personal affairs to someone outside your family, who would that person be?

Timothy must have been that person for Paul. In fact, we would be hard pressed to find someone the apostle Paul trusted more than Timothy. He was a coworker and one of Paul's closest friends. More than that, Timothy was a "son" to Paul.

While Timothy seems to have struggled with timidity, and others may have looked down on him because of his youthfulness, Paul recognized Timothy's potential. Timothy accompanied Paul on missionary journeys. The apostle left him in Ephesus to oversee the church there. So close were Timothy and Paul that both their names are listed as writers of numerous letters in the New Testament. On several occasions, Paul sent Timothy on critical missions to serve as his personal representative. As the apostle neared the end of his life and mission, he prepared his trusted son in the faith to be his successor in ministry.

Who are the people in your life who helped shape your self-image by their praise?

Are you investing in others in the same way? Explain.

Watch the video teaching for Session 6 to discover "The World of Timothy," then continue the group discussion.

FOCUS ATTENTION

What are one or two words you hope other people use to describe you?
Why are these character traits important to you?

EXPLORE THE TEXT

As a group, read Philippians 2:19.

What plans did Paul have for Timothy and why?

As a group, read Philippians 2:20-21.

Why did Paul plan to send Timothy rather than someone else?

What specific traits did Paul admire in Timothy?

Ask a volunteer to read Philippians 2:22-24.

Paul's statements concerning Timothy underscore his tremendous trust in him. Why could Paul put so much confidence in Timothy?

Paul noted that Timothy had proven his character over time. How can a person know about another person's character?

APPLY THE TEXT

Paul doled out strong praise for Timothy in this passage.

- Paul and Timothy were like-minded.

- Timothy genuinely cared about the church.

- Paul loved Timothy as a son.

- His character was proven because he had faithfully served alongside Paul.

Timothy exemplified the kind of Christian life Paul urged the Philippians to adopt; likewise, he exemplifies for us a life marked by Christlike humility and sacrificial service.

How can you be a model of humility and service to other Christians this week?

In what ways can you look out for the interests of Christ rather than your own interests?

What is the difference between false and genuine concern? Why is genuine concern for others an important trait for ministry?

Close your group time in prayer, reflecting on what you have discussed.

TIMOTHY

KEY VERSE

Don't let anyone despise your youth, but set an example for the believers in speech, in conduct, in love, in faith, and in purity."

— 1 Timothy 4:12

BASIC FACTS

1. Young ministry protégé of Paul who traveled with the apostle on two missionary journeys and took on several church leadership tasks in difficult settings.

2. Name *Timothy* is of Greek origin, meaning "honored of God" or "God-honorer."

3. Son of a Jewish Christian mother named Eunice and a Greek father (unnamed) from Lystra; grandmother's name was Lois.

4. Trained as a child to know the Scriptures and the way of salvation.

5. Sometimes lacked confidence in himself as a Christian leader.

TIMELINE

AD 30–40

- Jesus' ministry, crucifixion, resurrection, ascension 30–33
- Birth of the church during Pentecost 33
- Stephen's martyrdom 33
- Conversion of Saul (Paul) 33

AD 40–50

- Herod Agrippa I rules in Judea 41–44
- Barnabas brings Paul to Antioch 43
- Paul's first missionary journey 47–48
- Jerusalem Council 49
- Claudius expels Jews from Rome 49

KNOWN FOR

----

1. Because of Timothy's reputation among the believers of Lystra and Iconium, Paul recruited him to join the missionary team. Paul had Timothy circumcised to preempt the young man being rejected by Jewish audiences (Acts 16:1-3).

2. Paul trusted Timothy so thoroughly that he left the young leader in Berea to minister (Acts 17:13-14), and sent him in his stead to Macedonia (Acts 19:22), Thessalonica (1 Thess. 3:2), Corinth (1 Cor. 16:10), and Ephesus (1 Tim. 1:3).

3. Paul called Timothy his "true son in the faith," perhaps implying he had led Timothy to saving faith (1 Tim. 1:2). He also referred to Timothy as his most trusted and like-minded coworker in the gospel ministry to churches (Phil. 2:19-22).

4. Timothy spent a good deal of time as a pastor in Ephesus. During that time he received two letters from Paul (1 and 2 Timothy) that gave him encouragement and instruction for the church.

5. Like his spiritual mentor, Paul, Timothy may have spent some time in prison for the faith (Heb. 13:23).

6. The New Testament is silent about Timothy's death. One ancient church tradition posits that he remained the bishop of Ephesus until his martyrdom around the end of the first century.

AD 50–60

- Paul's second missionary journey 50–52
- Timothy joins Paul in Lystra 50
- Paul's third missionary journey 53–57
- Timothy works with Paul in Ephesus 54–56
- Paul arrested in Jerusalem; sent to Rome 57–59

AD 60–70

- Paul under house arrest in Rome 61–62
- Timothy returns to pastor in Ephesus at Paul's behest 62
- Paul writes 1 Timothy and Titus 62
- Paul writes 2 Timothy 67
- Apostle Paul martyred in Rome 67

Paul the Mentor

By Andreas J. Kostenberger

Timothy was in Ephesus, the third-largest city in the Roman Empire. In his first letter, Paul delineated Timothy's assignment: "instruct certain people not to teach false doctrine" (1 Tim. 1:3). At the outset, Paul referred to Timothy as his "true son in the faith" (v. 2). Earlier, he had said of Timothy, "I have no one else like-minded who will genuinely care about your interests" (Phil. 2:20). The expression "true son" could imply that Paul led Timothy to faith in Christ. However, "true son in the faith" most likely meant Timothy genuinely reproduced Paul's own spiritual characteristics, as a biological son would reflect his father's natural characteristics.

Paul's first letter to Timothy was written about fifteen years after their initial encounter. Since Timothy was likely a young man in his mid- or early twenties—Timothy's designation "disciple" implies independent adulthood—when he first met the apostle, Timothy would have been in his late thirties or early forties at the time of writing. Hence the reference to Timothy's "youth" (1 Tim. 4:12). Paul would have been in his early sixties.[1] The respective terms "apostle . . . son" therefore indicate both the different degrees of authority and the affectionate relationship between these two men of God. As his life and ministry began to wind down, Paul endeavored to preserve his legacy through his adoptive son in the faith. The phrase "true son" thus designates Timothy as Paul's rightful successor.

When Paul wrote his second letter to Timothy, a few years had passed since the first epistle. Timothy was still on assignment in Ephesus; Paul was no longer in Macedonia (1:3) but once again in prison, most likely in Rome (2 Tim. 1:8). Unlike his first imprisonment, where he stayed in his own rented house and received all who came to see him (see Acts 28:30), Paul was now suffering "to the point of being bound like a criminal" (2 Tim. 2:9) and was "being poured out as a drink offering" (4:6), meaning his death was imminent.

Paul was in a reminiscent mood (1:3-6) and the epistle assumed the character of a last testament in which Paul appealed to Timothy to "Preach the word . . . in season and out of season" (4:2) as he passed on the mantle of leadership to him. Although Paul

Andreas J. Kostenberger, "Paul the Mentor," *Biblical Illustrator*, Spring 2018.

urged Timothy to come to him "soon . . . before winter" (vv. 9,21), the text is unclear whether Paul saw him one last time. Timothy's role was particularly vital as many of Paul's associates had abandoned him by the time he wrote this second and final letter to Timothy (4:10-11,16). Paul's ministry was about to end; after his passing, his legacy would devolve to Timothy and other apostolic delegates such as Titus.

1. David W. Pao, "Let No One Despise Your Youth: Church and the World in the Pastoral Epistles," *Journal of the Evangelical Theological Society* 57, no. 4 (2014): 243–55.

The theater at Ephesus, built in the 3rd cent. BC. When Paul wrote Timothy, he reminded the young minister that he had sent him to Ephesus in order to "instruct certain people not to teach false doctrine or to pay attention to myths and endless genealogies" (1 Tim. 1:3, CSB).

Illustrator Photo/ Bob Schatz (11/35/16)

Read Acts 16:1-5.

Paul and Silas had begun the second missionary journey by traveling across Asia Minor, visiting the churches Paul and Barnabas had established on the first missionary journey (Acts 15:36-41). When the missionary team arrived in Lystra, they met a young Christian named Timothy. Although Luke, the writer of the Book of Acts, provided little information about Timothy's background, we learn that his family situation was unusual. Timothy's mother was a Jewish Christian, but his father was a Greek. Paul identified Timothy's mother as Eunice (2 Tim. 1:5).

Luke didn't give any details about the relationship between Timothy and his mother. Undoubtedly, she played a strong role in his spiritual development. Paul later wrote that Timothy had known the Scriptures since his infancy (2 Tim. 3:15). Surely he learned them from his mother.

Luke didn't report how Timothy became a Christian. Since Paul had come to Lystra on his first missionary journey, the young man could have been converted under Paul's influence (Acts 14:6-21). Paul elsewhere referred to Timothy as his son in the faith (Phil. 2:22; 1 Tim. 1:2).

Timothy had a good reputation among the Christians in the area of Lystra, and Paul invited him to join the missionary team (Acts 16:2). Paul must have seen great potential for missionary service in this young man. What we know of Timothy's later ministry demonstrates that Paul's confidence in Timothy was well-founded.

Paul knew, however, that this young man had not been circumcised as a baby. Jewish boys usually were circumcised on the eighth day of their lives, but Timothy's Gentile father had not followed this practice. To have a member of the missionary team be of Jewish lineage and yet uncircumcised would have hampered their ministry among the Jews. At the Jerusalem Council, Paul and others had insisted that circumcision was not essential for salvation (Acts 15:1-2,19). Paul had Timothy circumcised to facilitate his ministry among the Jews in the area, not to ensure Timothy's salvation.

What are some ways we can gain greater credibility among unbelievers so that we might be more effective in sharing the gospel with them?

Paul, Silas, and Timothy traveled from city to city, delivering the decisions of the Jerusalem Council (v. 4). Delivering the letter from the Jerusalem Council in the cities they visited reassured the Gentile believers and removed additional barriers to the gospel. The missionaries were not just delivering an edict but helping the churches grow in their faith and continue reaching the unbelievers around them (v. 5). The act of delivering the Jerusalem Council's message was a form of discipleship.

What was the two-fold outcome of the missionary team's visits?

What is our obligation to unbelievers, and what is our obligation to believers?

Our obligation to unbelievers is to share the gospel. Only the good news that Jesus saves can change lives; we are called to share this life-changing hope. Our ministry to believers is to strengthen their faith.

Paul must have been impressed with Timothy's abilities, because he left Timothy to pastor the church at Ephesus (1 Tim. 1:3-4). Paul eventually wrote two letters to Timothy to encourage him in his ministry. First and 2 Timothy are traditionally called the Pastoral Letters because a senior minister, Paul, wrote them to a younger minister, Timothy, about concerns of pastors.

What implication does Paul's seeing the potential in young Timothy have for you?

Read Philippians 2:19-24.

Timothy was with Paul and Silas when they planted the church at Philippi (Acts 16), and he was with Paul in Rome when Paul wrote to the Philippians approximately twelve years after starting the church there (Phil. 1:1). For years Timothy served the Lord faithfully at Paul's side. The long years of working with Timothy gave Paul complete assurance he could trust Timothy implicitly.

Paul hoped to visit the Philippian church soon, but he planned to send Timothy to them immediately. He couched his plans with a sincere, "I hope in the Lord Jesus." (Phil. 2:19). Paul didn't want to make plans and then ask God to bless them. He sincerely wanted to discern God's will.

Paul's purpose in sending Timothy to Philippi was first and foremost that the church could benefit from the presence of one of Paul's closest associates. Another purpose for sending Timothy was that Paul himself might be encouraged. Knowing the believers at Philippi were remaining faithful to Christ and were united would encourage Paul.

Paul had in Timothy someone who reflected his own desires accurately. Timothy would genuinely care about the Philippians' interests. He was not like others who sought their own interests. We can't be focused on others and on ourselves at the same time.

Which of your actions this week demonstrated that you are placing the interests of others ahead of your own. Which demonstrated that you are placing your own interests first?

The antidote to self-centeredness is always to look to the interests of Jesus Christ. New Testament writers consistently remind us of Jesus' example of service and sacrifice. In fact, in a rebuke to His disciples, Jesus said that to be the greatest in the kingdom, a Christian must serve others. He Himself was the ultimate example of this self-sacrifice (Mark 10:44-45).

The Philippians already knew Timothy's character. The Philippian Christians had observed Timothy in action and had firsthand knowledge of his proven character. That is, he had been tested and found to be genuine. In 2:7, Paul pointed out that Christ chose to be a servant; Timothy was following his Lord's example as one who served.

How does showing confidence in another person's character likely affect your relationship with that person?

We shouldn't be surprised that Paul spoke of his relationship with Timothy in terms of a father and his son. Paul had mentored Timothy in the faith. Timothy had served with Paul in the gospel ministry, at times accompanying the apostle, at times serving as an ambassador, and sometimes carrying letters. Paul genuinely loved Timothy and looked out for his best interests. So, if Paul couldn't go to the Philippians, he could send a trusted colleague like Timothy.

Who is your Timothy—your encourager, co-laborer, and friend in Christ? If you don't have a Timothy in your life, ask God to point you to someone who can encourage you in your spiritual journey.

As much as Paul wanted to send Timothy, however, he also needed to wait to see how things went with him (v. 23). Recall that Paul was writing from prison in Rome and awaiting trial before the emperor. When the verdict was in, he would send Timothy to Philippi. If Paul were found guilty, Timothy would represent him ably. Yet Paul was convinced in the Lord that he would be acquitted. When that happened, he quickly would arrange to visit the church.

Read 2 Timothy 1:3-6.

The Book of Acts ends with Paul in prison in Rome. The content of Paul's letters to Timothy and the tradition of the early church remind us that the Roman authorities released Paul after two years. After his release, Paul continued to engage in ministry, including writing the letters of 1 Timothy and Titus. Eventually, however, Paul was arrested again and imprisoned in Rome. The apostle likely wrote 2 Timothy during this second Roman imprisonment.

Second Timothy has been called Paul's "last will and testament." Paul knew his earthly pilgrimage would end shortly. At the same time, Paul continued to fulfill his gospel calling and sought to equip Timothy to carry on the work of the gospel after he was gone.

Although often imprisoned, Paul never viewed himself as a victim. He offered thanksgiving to God (2 Tim. 1:3). Paul's gratitude inspired him to remember Timothy in his prayers night and day.

Paul expressed his longing to see Timothy. This yearning was based on two factors. First, he remembered Timothy's tears (v. 4). Paul didn't explain the occasion for Timothy's emotion. It could have been the tearful farewell in Acts 20:37 when Paul parted from Timothy and the Ephesian elders. Timothy's tears underscored the friendship and esteem he and Paul held for each other. Second, Paul longed to see Timothy because he needed the joy that a reunion would bring. Paul knew that the source of true joy is Christ. He also knew that the joy of the Lord sometimes flows through a friend in Christ.

Paul was thoroughly convinced of Timothy's sincere faith. Ultimately, believers in Lystra and the neighboring town of Iconium saw the same character in Timothy and affirmed the sincere faith evident in him too (see Acts 16:1-2).

How persuaded are you that you have a "sincere faith"?

Paul traced Timothy's faith back to its roots. Timothy's grandmother Lois had demonstrated such faith. His mother Eunice provided a similar example. Timothy's mother and grandmother taught Timothy the Scriptures from infancy (2 Tim. 3:15). Their teachings greatly influenced his life.

Having a strong Christian family is important, but Paul knew that more important was a personal relationship with Jesus. Having godly parents and grandparents is important, but their faith cannot substitute for an individual's own faith in Jesus as Savior.

What benefit did Paul want Timothy to gain by remembering his spiritual heritage? How is a person's spiritual growth impacted by the lives of others?

Timothy had the knowledge of his mother's and grandmother's faith to guide and encourage him. He had the affirmation of the believers in Lystra and Iconium. He had the affirmation of Paul through the laying on of his hands. He had his own history of ministry experiences recounted in Acts and noted elsewhere in Paul's Letters. He had the personal, spiritual experience of receiving and fulfilling a Spirit-empowered call to ministry. Yet even with all of these examples and experiences to draw on, Timothy needed a reminder to "rekindle the gift of God" (v. 6). This expression presents an image of fanning, stirring, and feeding a fire to keep it burning intently.

Paul's counsel to Timothy reminds us that even strong persons can become weary, and even faithful individuals can become discouraged. Even people of sincere faith need an occasional spiritual checkup, an encouragement to reflect on their ministry to confirm that they are living out the faith to which God called them. We all need the prayers and encouragements of others and the periodic reminder to fan the fire of our faith that we may render our best service to God.

TIPS FOR LEADING A SMALL GROUP

Follow these guidelines to prepare for each group session.

PRAYERFULLY PREPARE

Review

Review the weekly material and group questions ahead of time.

Pray

Be intentional about praying for each person in the group. Ask the Holy Spirit to work through you and the group discussion as you point to Jesus each week through God's Word.

MINIMIZE DISTRACTIONS

Create a comfortable environment. If group members are uncomfortable, they'll be distracted and therefore not engaged in the group experience. Plan ahead by considering these details:

Seating

Temperature

Lighting

Food or Drink

Surrounding Noise

General Cleanliness

At best, thoughtfulness and hospitality show guests and group members they're welcome and valued in whatever environment you choose to gather. At worst, people may never notice your effort, but they're also not distracted. Do everything in your ability to help people focus on what's most important: connecting with God, with the Bible, and with one another.

INCLUDE OTHERS

Your goal is to foster a community in which people are welcome just as they are but encouraged to grow spiritually. Always be aware of opportunities to include any people who visit the group and to invite new people to join your group. An inexpensive way to make first-time guests feel welcome or to invite someone to get involved is to give them their own copies of this Bible study book.

ENCOURAGE DISCUSSION

A good small-group experience has the following characteristics.

Everyone Participates

Encourage everyone to ask questions, share responses, or read aloud.

No One Dominates—Not Even the Leader

Be sure that your time speaking as a leader takes up less than half of your time together as a group. Politely guide discussion if anyone dominates.

Nobody Is Rushed Through Questions

Don't feel that a moment of silence is a bad thing. People often need time to think about their responses to questions they've just heard or to gain courage to share what God is stirring in their hearts.

Input Is Affirmed and Followed Up

Make sure you point out something true or helpful in a response. Don't just move on. Build community with follow-up questions, asking how other people have experienced similar things or how a truth has shaped their understanding of God and the Scripture you're studying. People are less likely to speak up if they fear that you don't actually want to hear their answers or that you're looking for only a certain answer.

God and His Word Are Central

Opinions and experiences can be helpful, but God has given us the truth. Trust God's Word to be the authority and God's Spirit to work in people's lives. You can't change anyone, but God can. Continually point people to the Word and to active steps of faith.

HOW TO USE THE LEADER GUIDE

PREPARE TO LEAD

Each session of the Leader Guide is designed to be torn out so you, the leader, can have this front-and-back page with you as you lead your group through the session. Watch the session teaching video and read through the session content with the Leader Guide tear-out in hand and notice how it supplements each section of the study.

FOCUS ATTENTION

These questions are provided to help get the discussion started. They are generally more introductory and topical in nature.

EXPLORE THE TEXT

Questions in this section have some sample answers or discussion prompts provided in the Leader Guide, if needed, to help you jump-start or steer the conversation.

APPLY THE TEXT

This section contains questions that allow group members an opportunity to apply the content they have been discussing together.

BIOGRAPHY AND FURTHER INSIGHT MOMENT

These sections aren't covered in the leader guide and may be used during the group session or by group members as a part of the personal study time during the week. If you choose to use them during your group session, make sure you are familiar with the content and how you intend to use it before your group meets.

Conclude each group session with a prayer.

SESSION 1 | LEADER GUIDE

FOCUS ATTENTION

Which song title best describes you: "Rock the Boat" or "Peace Like a River"? If you like to keep peace at all costs, what kind of situation would cause you to rock the boat?

- Because some Christians are naturally timid and/or don't like to confront or be confronted by others, they have never boldly declared their Christian beliefs and values. Others feel their beliefs are a private matter. Both types of people are unwilling to take risks regarding their faith. Some situations, however, call for believers to exhibit risky boldness in declaring their faith.

EXPLORE THE TEXT

Ask a volunteer to read Acts 6:8-10.

What uniquely qualified Stephen for his ministry? What do verses 3 and 5 add to your understanding of his qualification? How were those qualities needed for Stephen to do what he did?

- Stephen was full of the Holy Spirit, wisdom, faith (vv. 3,5) and God's grace and power (v. 8).

- Full of God and not of himself, Stephen relied on God's power, not his own abilities.

- The Spirit filled Stephen with great wisdom and bold confidence in sharing the gospel so that his opponents were unable to resist the truth he spoke.

Ask a volunteer to read Acts 6:11-15.

What uniquely qualified Stephen for his ministry? What do verses 3 and 5 add to your understanding of his qualification? How were those qualities needed for Stephen to do what he did?

- Although Stephen had been faithful in his witness to Jesus' teachings, the men who had argued with him twisted his words and incited the crowd against him, effectively stirring up a riot.

What unfairness did Stephen endure? Once the situation turned hostile, what might Stephen have been tempted to do?

- Stephen could have backed off his bold claims in fear or for self–preservation. Instead, he stayed the course. He remained bold amid hostility.

Ask a volunteer to read Acts 7:51-53.

What accusations did Stephen make against his accusers? Do you think his words were too harsh? Explain.

- Stephen boldly defended himself by taking the offensive. He accused the men of resisting the Holy Spirit, persecuting and killing God's prophets, killing the Messiah, and not keeping God's law.

Ask a volunteer to read Acts 7:54-60.

Which of these verses elicits strong emotion for you? Why? How is this part of Stephen's story a different kind of boldness than in the previous verses?

- Stephen didn't simply speak with boldness; he lived boldly in a situation where many would have crumbled in fear. The Holy Spirit's presence and power in his life equipped him to remain faithful to the very end.

APPLY THE TEXT

Are you willing to ask God to make you bold for the gospel to the point that you will unashamedly share the message of Jesus regardless of the consequences? Why or why not?

What sacrifices is God calling you to make right now for the sake of the gospel?

What does Stephen's martyrdom teach about how God wants us to define success?

SESSION 2 | LEADER GUIDE

FOCUS ATTENTION

Share about a life-changing experience. Describe your life before and after the life change.

- An unexpected encounter with Jesus completely changed Saul's life. He went from persecuting believers to being known as Paul, a champion for Christ.

- A commitment to Christ leads to life change.

EXPLORE THE TEXT

Ask a volunteer to read Acts 9:1-9.

Take a look at the way Jesus interacted with Saul (Paul) in this passage. Beyond the blinding light, how did He get Saul's attention?

- Jesus spoke personally to Saul by name.

- Jesus identified Himself and gave Saul directions. He didn't tell Saul specifically what to do, just to move ahead for further instructions. Saul was obedient and went as Jesus directed.

How was Saul (Paul) immediately changed by his encounter with Jesus? How do you think his companions might have responded to the change?

- God caused Saul to be temporarily blind, which might have been a symbol for Saul's spiritual darkness.

- Saul couldn't eat or drink for three days, possibly because he was too upset by his experience.

- In an instant, Saul changed from a powerful man on his way to arrest others, to a helpless individual who had to be led by his companions.

Ask a volunteer to read Acts 9:10-19a.

The Lord called Saul His "chosen instrument" (v. 15). What does it mean to be chosen by God?

- God chose Saul to carry the gospel to Gentiles, kings, and Israelites. His commissioning message included suffering.

- God uses all kinds of people in kingdom work and does so in different ways. Notice how He used Saul's traveling companions, Ananias, and Saul himself.

- God calls people to be His messengers. The first step is a commitment to follow Christ. Saul was baptized and began proclaiming Jesus.

What significant things happened in Paul's life after Ananias prayed for him?

- After Ananias prayed for Paul, Paul regained his sight, was baptized, and regained his strength.

Ask a volunteer to read Acts 9:19b-21.

In what ways did Paul demonstrate his new commitment to Jesus?

- Paul spent time with the disciples in Damascus and immediately began to share his faith in Jesus in the synagogues.

What would people have expected Paul to say when he came to the synagogue? What was the reaction of the people who heard Paul proclaiming the name of Jesus?

- When Paul first arrived in the synagogues after his conversion experience, the people must have expected him to try to disprove the claims the Christians were making. So they were astonished that this man who had killed Christians was now himself professing faith in the name of Jesus.

APPLY THE TEXT

Do you assume some people are beyond God's reach? How does the account of Saul's conversion challenge those assumptions?

Recall a time when God got your attention. What were the circumstances?

Who is someone in your life, like Ananias, who has helped you on your spiritual journey?

SESSION 3 | LEADER GUIDE

FOCUS ATTENTION

Do you look at the glass as half-empty or half-full? Why? Who is the most positive person you know? What does he or she do to make you think that?

- Some believers seem to have a good word for everyone they meet, while others are critical and see only the faults of those around them. Our personalities and past experiences are no excuse; God wants all of His people to take positive actions that will help them be a source of encouragement to one another. Barnabas was that type of person.

EXPLORE THE TEXT

Ask a volunteer to read Acts 11:19-22.

Why might the church in Jerusalem have sent Barnabas to Antioch?

- The church in Jerusalem had praised God over the salvation of Gentiles in Acts 11:18.
- Barnabas was a known encourager. (See Acts 4:36-37; 9:27; 15:37-39.)

Ask a volunteer to read Acts 11:23-24.

Other than the fact that he had the reputation of being an encourager, what about Barnabas led the church at Jerusalem to select him to report to them?

- "He was a good man" and "full of the Holy Spirit and faith," just like Stephen (Acts 6:5). When Barnabas arrived in Antioch, far from criticizing the new undertaking, he was able to see the grace of God at work in all the Gentile conversions, and he rejoiced.
- The strength of Barnabas's character gave the church in Jerusalem confidence in him to evaluate this new work of the Lord in Antioch.

Ask a volunteer to read Acts 11:25-26.

Knowing Barnabas's character, why do you think he recruited Paul's help? What work was there for Barnabas and Paul to do in Antioch?

- Barnabas searched for Paul in Tarsus. He had encouraged Paul once before (see 9:27) and knew his potential. Barnabas recognized the Gentile believers in Antioch gave an opportunity for Paul to lead as God had called him (9:15).

- A large number of new believers needed to be discipled.

Ask a volunteer to read Acts 11:27-30.

What fears could have gripped the church on hearing the news from Agabus? What happened instead?

- A severe famine was coming. Christians were already being persecuted for their faith, and a famine could greatly add to the uncertainties they faced.

- The church in Antioch sent Barnabas and Paul to Jerusalem with aid for the Christians in Judea.

Does it seem strange to you that a young church would send aid to one that is already established? Explain. What does this fact tell you about the Christians in Antioch?

- The young church learned from the encouragement they received and was now ready to offer encouragement to others.

APPLY THE TEXT

In the early stages of your relationship with Christ, who encouraged you to persevere? How did he or she do that?

In what way(s) can you encourage a new believer or new church member this week?

In what way(s) can you follow the example of verses 27-30 this week and help a fellow believer who is in a difficult situation?

SESSION 4 | LEADER GUIDE

FOCUS ATTENTION

**What are some of the rules you're expected to follow in your daily routine?
What are some of the "extra-biblical" rules we place on new believers?**

EXPLORE THE TEXT

Ask a volunteer to read Acts 15:1-5.

**Who came to Antioch from Jerusalem, and what were they teaching?
How did Paul and Barnabas respond, and what did the church propose?**

- Believers from Judea began to teach the Christians that circumcision was required for salvation.

- Paul and Barnabas debated with them and were sent to the apostles and elders in Jerusalem to discuss the controversy.

Ask a volunteer to read Acts 15:6-11.

What significance did the gospel being inclusive of different people groups have for the Jews? the Gentiles?

- God created all people, and He sent His Son to purchase salvation for anyone who believes in Him.

- Since God saves all believers regardless of their ethnicity, we are reminded that we are to be witnesses of the gospel "in Jerusalem, in all Judea and Samaria, and to the ends of the earth" (Acts 1:8).

Ask a volunteer to read Acts 15:19-23.

What was James's recommendation? How did his judgment satisfy both parties?

- James announced his opinion, perhaps as a formal motion: Gentiles would not have to become Jewish converts to become Christians (v. 19).

- Then James suggested a letter be sent to Gentile churches instructing believers to keep four ritual requirements in deference to Jewish Christians.

What is the significance of the four actions prohibited?

- As believers, our testimonies are effective when we avoid idolatry and immorality. This is why the letter from the Jerusalem Council listed four things to avoid and mentioned that the Gentile believers would do well if they did indeed avoid those things.

- By being sensitive to the beliefs and practices of Jews, Gentile Christians might reach them.

Ask a volunteer to read Acts 15:30-31.

The messengers arrived in Antioch and read the letter, reporting the council's decision. How might the letter (recorded in vv. 23-29) have been encouraging to Gentile believers (v. 31)?

- They rejoiced that salvation is a result of grace alone, not grace plus works.

- This was the news the mostly Gentile church had waited for. They had a spiritual question and needed help. The leaders in the Jerusalem church were able to give direction and encouragement.

APPLY THE TEXT

Are there any signs that your church or Bible study group has turned its focus inward, instead of focusing on people who are far from God? What are those signs?

How might you or your church unintentionally make it harder for a believer who has just turned to Christ?

What lessons can you learn from James about dealing with distractions that take the church's focus off the main thing—the gospel?

SESSION 5 | LEADER GUIDE

FOCUS ATTENTION

In what subject would you be a good tutor? In what subject do you feel inadequate? Explain.

- Priscilla and Aquila serve as examples of ways we can help people who have an incomplete understanding of the Christian faith.

EXPLORE THE TEXT

Ask a volunteer to read Acts 18:24-26.

What words give you clues about Apollos's skills and giftings? What are the different ways believers respond to people who are confident and gifted communicators?

- Apollos was a bold, eloquent speaker who knew the Scriptures well. His presentation was fervent.

- Some believers are mesmerized or intimidated by such bold confidence, keeping quiet because they think that person knows more than they do. Others gossip or are quietly critical of inaccuracies or an incomplete understanding of Christianity. Still others, like Priscilla and Aquila, lovingly support and hold such people accountable for presenting the gospel accurately.

What concern did Priscilla and Aquila have with Apollos and his teaching? What can we learn from the way Aquila and Priscilla confronted Apollos?

- Apollos only knew of John's baptism. With limited knowledge of Jesus' life, death, and resurrection and the coming of the Holy Spirit, his understanding of Christianity was incomplete.

- Aquila and Priscilla didn't ruin Apollos's testimony by publicly correcting him; rather, they took him home and privately helped him with what he needed to know.

- People are more receptive to new truth when we take the time to establish a personal relationship with them, spend time with them, and have meaningful conversations with them.

- Listening to what people say about Christianity will help us know how complete their understanding is and how to help them.

Why is a limited understanding of the gospel and the Christian faith a dangerous proposition?

- Without full disclosure, a bad decision can be made with limited information available. A proper understanding of something is necessary before we can draw reasonable conclusions.

- When Christians don't have a complete understanding of the gospel, they could potentially confuse other believers based upon their limited knowledge. That is why knowledgeable Christians should come alongside new believers to explain the truths about God.

Ask a volunteer to read Acts 18:27-28.

How did God use the church in Ephesus to minister to Apollos?

- The congregation in Ephesus encouraged Apollos to go to Achaia by writing a letter to the believers there instructing them to welcome him as a fellow believer.

- Christians today can help ministers and missionaries by encouraging them to pursue their desire to share the gospel with others.

What was the end result of Priscilla and Aquila's actions on behalf of Apollos?

- Apollos went on to help believers in Corinth.

- He boldly preached that Jesus is the Messiah. Apollos was able to publicly refute the Jews in a debate about the claims of Christ as Messiah. He pointed the Jews to various Old Testament prophecies that were fulfilled with the coming of Christ.

- Arguably, none of this would have been possible if not for the faithfulness of Aquila and Priscilla.

APPLY THE TEXT

If someone came to you with an incomplete understanding of Christianity, would you help him or send him to someone else? Why?

What gifts do you feel you might have that God has given you for Christian service? Where do you sense God has equipped you to serve?

SESSION 6 | LEADER GUIDE

FOCUS ATTENTION

What are one or two words you hope other people use to describe you? Why are these character traits important to you?

- Paul began Philippians 2 by challenging the Philippians to a life of unselfishness, humility, and unity by holding up Jesus' example of humility and sacrifice.

- Paul offered Timothy, his younger co-laborer, as an example of Christ's mindset of humility and sacrifice.

EXPLORE THE TEXT

Ask a volunteer to read Philippians 2:19.

What plans did Paul have for Timothy and why?

- Paul, writing from prison in Rome, expressed his intention to send Timothy on a mission to Philippi as soon as he got news of the settlement of his case.

- The purpose of Timothy's visit was so that Paul and the Philippians would be mutually encouraged by news concerning each other. Timothy's visit would benefit both the Philippian church and Paul.

Ask a volunteer to read Philippians 2:20-21.

Why did Paul plan to send Timothy rather than someone else?

- Paul wished to send the most able person; Timothy was the most qualified.

- In sending Timothy, Paul sent the best he had—an extension of himself. Sending Timothy would help prevent the Philippians from being disappointed that Paul himself was not coming. Paul expressed his full confidence in Timothy's ability in the matter.

What specific traits did Paul admire in Timothy?

- Timothy showed concern for others. He put others' needs ahead of his own self-interest.

- When you look out for the interests of others, you look out for the interests of Christ.

- Timothy was a living testimony of the kind of Christian Paul was instructing the Philippians to be (2:4). More importantly, Timothy lived out the humble, self-giving life Christ had exemplified (2:5-8).

Ask a volunteer to read Philippians 2:22-24.

Paul's statements concerning Timothy underscore his tremendous trust in him. Why could Paul put so much confidence in Timothy?

- The years Timothy and Paul spent together showed Paul that he and Timothy shared a mutual passion for reaching people for Christ and establishing healthy churches throughout their world.

Paul noted that Timothy had proven his character over time. How can a person know about another person's character?

- The best way is the same way Paul knew about Timothy's character— from his proven track record.

APPLY THE TEXT

How can you be a model of humility and service to other Christians this week?

In what ways can you look out for the interests of Christ rather than your own interests?

What is the difference between false and genuine concern? Why is genuine concern for others an important trait for ministry?

When he arrived and saw
the grace of God, he was glad
and encouraged all of them to
remain true to the Lord with
devoted hearts.

ACTS 11:23

Whether you're a new Christian or you have believed in Jesus for several years, the people of the Bible have so much wisdom to offer. For that reason, we have created additional resources for churches that want to maximize the reach and impact of the *Characters* studies.

Complete Series Leader Pack

Want to take your group through the whole *Explore the Bible: Characters* series? You'll want a *Complete Series Leader Pack*. This *Pack* includes *Leader Kits* from Volume 1 - Volume 7. It allows you to take your group from The Patriarchs all the way to The Early Church Leaders.

$179.99

Video Bundle for Groups

All video sessions are available to purchase as a downloadable bundle.

$60.00

eBooks

A digital version of the *Bible Study Book* is also available for those who prefer studying with a phone or tablet. Some churches also find eBooks easier to distribute to study participants.

Starter Packs

You can save money and time by purchasing starter packs for your group or church. Every *Church Starter Pack* includes a digital *Church Launch Kit* and access to a digital version of the *Leader Kit* videos.

$99.99 | **Single Group Starter Pack**
(10 *Bible Study Books*, 1 *Leader Kit*)

$449.99 | **Small Church Starter Pack**
(50 *Bible Study Books*, 5 *Leader Kit* DVDs, and access to video downloads)

$799.99 | **Medium Church Starter Pack**
(100 *Bible Study Books*, 10 *Leader Kit* DVDs, and access to video downloads)

$3495.99 | **Large Church Starter Pack**
(500 *Bible Study Books*, 50 *Leader Kit* DVDs, and access to video downloads)

LifeWay.com/characters
Order online or call 800.458.2772.

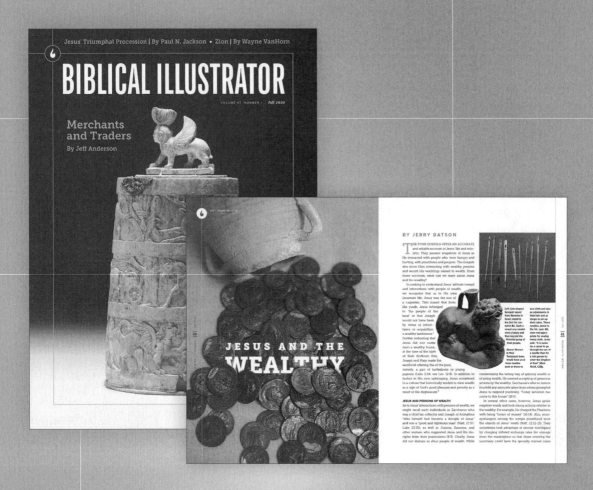

EXPLORE THE BIBLE.

WHERE TO GO
FROM HERE

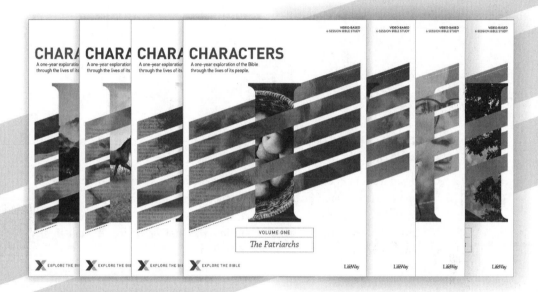

We hope you've enjoyed learning about some of the characters of Scripture. If you'd like to go even deeper in study, we recommend Explore the Bible. This ongoing series is designed to illuminate the historical, cultural, and biblical context of Scripture—book by book.

For more information, call 800.458.2772 or visit goexplorethebible.com

EXPLORE YOUR OPTIONS

EXPLORE THE BIBLE.

EXPLORE THE BIBLE

If you want to understand the Bible in its historical, cultural, and biblical context, few resources offer the thoroughness of the Explore the Bible ongoing quarterly curriculum. Over the course of nine years, you can study the whole truth, book by book, in a way that's practical, sustainable, and age appropriate for your entire church.

6- TO 8-WEEK STUDIES

If you're looking for short-term resources that are more small-group friendly, visit the LifeWay website to see Bible studies from a variety of noteworthy authors, including Ravi Zacharias, J.D. Greear, Matt Chandler, David Platt, Tony Evans, and many more.

Prices and availability subject to change without notice.